THE WISDOM OF ISLAM

ROBERT FRAGER Ph.D.

THE WISDOM
OF WISDOM
OF ISLAM

An introduction to
the living experience
of Islamic belief and practice

ROBERT FRAGER Ph.D.

BARRON'S

DEDICATION

I dedicate this book to my teacher and elder brother on the Path of Truth, Sheikh Tosun Bayrak al-Jerrahi al-Halveti, whose wisdom has guided and inspired me for over twenty years.

First edition for the United States, its territories and dependencies, and Canada published exclusively by Barron's Educational Series, Inc.

© 2002 Godsfield Press
Text © 2002 Robert Frager

Produced exclusively for Barron's Educational Series, Inc. by Godsfield Press. Designed for Godsfield Press by The Bridgewater Book Company

Map illustrations Andrew Farmer

All inquiries should be addressed to:
Barron's Educational Series, Inc.
250 Wireless Boulevard
Hauppauge, NY 11788
http://www.barronseduc.com

ISBN 0-7641-2254-1
Library of Congress Catalog Card No. 2001099031

Robert Frager asserts the moral right to be identified as the author of this work.

Printed and bound in China

9 8 7 6 5 4 3 2 1

NOTE FOR READER: USE OF HONORIFICS
Traditional Islamic usage calls for an honorific following the names of the Prophets and Saints each time they are mentioned. For example: Prophet Muhammad (peace and blessings upon him) or the Prophets Abraham, Moses, and Jesus (God's peace be upon them). This book uses the following traditional Arabic calligraphy rather than English words to signify these honorifics:

ﷺ = peace and blessings upon him

علیه السلام = peace be upon them

CONTENTS

INTRODUCTION

Islam is a mystery to most Westerners. And yet, Islam has contributed to Western thought and culture for over a thousand years. Judaism, Christianity, and Islam are all monotheistic faiths, the roots of which go back to the Prophet Abraham عليه السلام [1]. The Qur'an clearly states that Islam is not a new teaching, but a continuation of the perennial Truth that was taught earlier by Moses, Jesus, and other great prophets عليه السلام.

> We believe in God
> And in what has been sent down to us,
> What has been revealed to Abraham and Ishmael
> And Isaac and Jacob and their offspring,
> And what was given to Moses and to Jesus
> And all other prophets by the Lord.
> We make no distinction among them.
>
> (Qur'an 11:136)

Two thirds of the chapters of the Qur'an include references to the events of the Bible and the biblical prophets, including Adam, Eve, Abraham, Noah, Jonah, Moses, Aaron, David, and Solomon عليه السلام. The Qur'an also mentions with reverence John the Baptist, Mary, and Jesus عليه السلام. For Muslims, the Qur'an is the revealed Word of God. As Christians believe God came to Earth in Jesus, Muslims believe the Qur'an is God's Word sent down

Far right: Crowds fill the main hall at Istiqial Mosque, or the Shalat, the largest mosque in Southeast Asia, central Jakarta, Indonesia.

to Earth. In Islam, Muhammad ﷺ is revered as a great prophet and an exemplary human being, but he is in no way considered divine.

There is no ordained priesthood in Islam. All Muslims enjoy equal access to God. The imam is the prayer leader in each congregation, the one who has the greatest knowledge of the Qur'an. This is less true for the minority Shiah tradition, which invests greater authority in its mullahs or religious leaders. In contrast to Christianity, there is no original sin in Islam. Just the opposite is held to be true. A human being is the highest form of God's Creation, meant to serve as God's deputy on Earth.

"And Lo! Your Lord said to the angels, 'Behold, I am about to establish upon Earth one who shall rule it'" (Qur'an 2:30).

THE CREED OF FAITH

The fundamental beliefs of Islam are summarized in the following creed:

> I believe in God,
>
> and in God's angels,
>
> and in the Holy Books,
>
> and in God's Messengers,
>
> and in the Day of Resurrection,
>
> and in destiny,
>
> that all good and bad come from God,
>
> and that there is life after this life.

The first article of faith is the belief that there is one God, that God is both transcendent of Creation and also imminent; God's Attributes are present in all things. God is before the before and after the after, beyond our comprehension. God is complete and perfect. The Sufis, the mystics of Islam, teach that God can be found in the heart. They are particularly fond of a famous *hadith qudsi*, an extra-Qur'anic revelation from God speaking through the Prophet Muhammad ﷺ: "I, Who cannot be fit into all the universes upon universes, fit in the heart of the loving believer."

The second article of faith holds that the angels are instruments of God's Will. They form a series of ever more luminous beings, a hierarchy between humanity and God. Humans have both an angelic nature and an animal nature. The Prophet ﷺ said, "God created the angels from intellect without sensuality, the beasts from sensuality without intellect, and humanity from both intellect and sensuality. So when our intellect overcomes our sensuality, we are better than the angels, but when our sensuality overcomes our intellect, we are worse than the beasts."

The third article of faith is belief in four great books: the Torah brought by Moses, the Psalms of David, the Gospels inspired by Jesus ﷺ, and the Qur'an revealed to Muhammad ﷺ. There have also been hundreds of shorter scriptures, or "scrolls," revealed to other prophets.

According to the fourth article of faith, each prophet brought the same truth from the same divine source, and therefore we honor and believe in all of them.

The fifth article of faith reminds us we are here on Earth to learn and to grow.

When the Day of Resurrection comes, God will examine everyone's life. It is the balance between the good and bad we have done in our lives that will determine our place in the afterlife.

The sixth article of faith is belief in destiny or fate. That is, nothing happens purely by chance, nothing happens without God's Will.

The seventh article holds that all things come from God, including those things we perceive as good or pleasant, and those we view as bad or unpleasant.

The eighth article teaches that life does not end with death. In many ways, life in this world is like a dream, and our true life begins in the next world.

Most people in the world agree with these basic beliefs. Islam holds that all religions teach the same essential truths, as all religions originate from the same divine source. My Sufi master often commented, "There is only one religion. Because there is only one God."

"You are not a believer until you wish for others that which you wish for yourself."
Muhammad ﷺ 2

CHAPTER ONE

THE FIVE PILLARS OF ISLAM

There are five basic practices in Islam. These five pillars are: bearing witness, prayer, fasting, charity, and pilgrimage. These religious disciplines are rooted in the teachings of the Qur'an and in the example of the Prophet Muhammad ﷺ. You enter into Islam by reciting that there is no god but God. In addition, all Muslims are to pray five times a day, fast during Ramadan, give annual charity, and make the Hajj, or pilgrimage.

THE FIRST PILLAR
BEARING WITNESS

Previous page: Pilgrims praying at the Ka'bah in Makkah.

Entrance into Islam begins with the following recitation: "I bear witness that there is no god but God, and I bear witness that Muhammad is a servant and a Messenger of God." These words are recited into an infant's ear after birth. Recitation of this formula is a necessary and also sufficient condition for becoming a Muslim as an adult. When you accept God, you take God as the greatest influence in your life. Following God's Will and doing that which pleases God become more important than anything else, including the demands of your body and your ego. When you acknowledge Muhammad ﷺ as God's Messenger, you pledge to follow his teachings because those teachings came from God.

How can we "bear witness" to the truth that there is but one God? How do we "witness" that Muhammad ﷺ brought God's Message to the world? To know that there is one God is to know firsthand the unity of God. To hear about something is to gain secondhand knowledge. To see, or witness, is to experience for oneself. Paradoxically, this act of witnessing represents both the beginning of Islam and the goal of Islamic spirituality.

The phrase *La ilaha ilAllah* (There is no god but God) literally means "No gods, there is God." It urges us to worship God alone, and to avoid worshiping the transitory things of this world. Many of us worship fame, money, pleasure, or security—and then we live our lives seeking these things instead of seeking God. People of the past worshiped idols and believed there was real spiritual power in a clay statue. Today, we have made idols of material success. Like those who worshiped a clay figure as if it were divine, we confuse the fleeting for the eternal.

To declare that "Muhammad ﷺ is a servant and a Messenger of God" does not exclude our love and reverence for other great prophets. The Qur'an teaches that God sent down a prophet to every people, to every tribe or community, to teach God's Message throughout the world. All the great prophets have been God's devoted servants. They dedicated themselves to serving God and set aside their own wills and their own wants and needs in order to manifest God's Will as perfectly as possible.

My Sufi teacher, Sheikh Muzaffer, taught that all the prophets and messengers brought the same truth as they were all filled with the same divine light and wisdom. In a room lit by several lamps there is only one, indivisible light.

A young Muslim is learning to pray by accompanying his father to the mosque and joining the congregation.

THE SECOND PILLAR
DAILY PRAYER

Observant Muslims heed the call to prayer five times a day. They respond to the following exhortation:

God is greater. God is greater.
God is greater. God is greater.
I bear witness that there is no god but God.
I bear witness that there is no god but God.
I bear witness that Muhammad is a servant
and a Messenger of God.
I bear witness that Muhammad is a servant
and a Messenger of God.
Come to prayer, come to prayer.
Come to felicity, come to felicity.
God is greater. God is greater.
There is no god but God.

The sentence "God is greater" (*Allahu akbar*) is stronger than "God is great." After all, we might say that many things are great. To say "God is greater" is to remind ourselves that no matter how great anything in this world is, God is still greater. It reminds us there is nothing even remotely comparable to God.

Daily prayer occurs just before sunrise, just after noon, later afternoon, shortly after sunset, and after dark. Muslims can pray at home or any place that is clean, but it is considered better to pray in congregation in a mosque. Men and women line up separately, standing in straight lines, shoulder to shoulder. All who come to the mosque pray together, without regard to wealth or status. A beggar might pray next to a king.

Prayer begins by facing Makkah, putting our hands up to our ears, palms forward, saying, *Allahu akbar.* In raising our hands, we try to put the world and all our worldly concerns behind us. If we open our hearts, we can feel ourselves in the presence of God, with nothing between us and God. It may be hard to put aside the world completely, but we try.

> "Pray as if God were standing before you,
> for although you do not see God, God always sees you."
> Muhammad ﷺ [1]

Each prayer is done in *rakahs*, or cycles. A single cycle involves standing and reciting one or two passages from the Qur'an, then bowing, straightening up, and kneeling and bowing twice. In every *rakah*, the first recitation consists of the first surah (chapter) of the Qur'an, *surah Fatihah. Al-Fatihah* means the Opening. It opens the Qur'an and it can also open our hearts. (For an interpretation of this surah, see Chapter 3.)

> In the Name of God, Most Gracious, Most Merciful:
> All praise is due to God alone, the Sustainer
>   of all the Worlds.
> Most Gracious, Most Merciful,
> Lord of the Day of Judgment.
> You alone do we worship, and to You alone
>   do we turn for help.
> Guide us along the straight path—
> The path of those whom you have blessed, not of those
>   who have been condemned [by You], nor of those
>   who go astray. (1:1–7)

At night, the muezzin (a Muslim official) gives the call to prayer from a minaret high above the city.

THE THIRD PILLAR
FASTING

A Muslim family and their guests enjoying fast break together.

During the lunar month of Ramadan, all Muslims who are able to do so fast every day from before dawn to sunset. During the day, we abstain from eating, drinking, smoking, having sex, and arguing and fighting. This is a demanding practice, designed to help us to become more aware of the conflicting forces of our lower and higher natures. Our material nature constantly seeks material gratification—from all of material Creation. Our spiritual nature seeks only one thing—God.

We often give in immediately to the demands of our bodies. Whenever we are hungry, we rush to grab some food. When we are thirsty, we find something to drink at once. By opposing the demands of the body during fasting, we strengthen our will. At a deeper level, we also remind ourselves that we have the capacity to ignore our inner

Fasting for the First Time

"The difficult part of daytime fasting is not the lack of nourishment. (Every night, starting at sunset, one must eat.) It is the willed postponement of satisfaction. A fast calls normal behavior into question. The mechanics of appetite are broken up. The mouth waters, the hand reaches. A shadow falls between response and need.

"This was my first Ramadan as a Muslim. . . . Beginning had been the worst part. To restrict one's intake after a fixed date, then maintain a month-long siege against it took the nerve of a soldier going to battle. I began to see the fast as a war [between my thirst and my desire to fast]. Self-respect lay on the line every time I salivated. Food was hard to forget and a pain to remember. I looked at a clock and was always amazed. When time didn't drag, it raced.

"The hardships of fasting are easy to describe. The benefits were more subtle. Days passed before I noticed. Beyond the obvious gnawing gut, I began to feel a surprising independence. The sensation was indefinable at first. Later relief came into it as I saw that survival did not depend on steady streams of food. The fast did not become easier with time. I napped late [after morning prayer] and occasionally was dizzy. My energy flagged every afternoon. Only I noticed less the difficulties. More and more my light-headedness was accompanied by a sweet taste in the mouth." [2]

demands for material gratification. It is both a pleasure and a duty to perform a practice that pleases God.

For the Sufis, fasting is a spiritual discipline, a discipline of inner purification as well as outer asceticism. The Sufi sage Abu Hamid al-Ghazzali described three levels of fasting:

The fasting of the average Muslim involves refraining from satisfying the appetite of the stomach and the desire for sex.

The fasting of the Sufi is to keep the ears, the eyes, the tongue, and the hands free from sin or harmful actions.

The fasting of the saint is the fast of the heart, that is, to fast from all worldly concerns and to think only of God.

THE PROPHET SAID —ON RAMADAN

The Prophet ﷺ gave the following sermon on the first day of Ramadan:

Holy Ramadan, the best of all months, is here today. . . .God Most High has made it obligatory to fast during the days of this month and made it voluntary to pass the nights in prayer. . . .

During the first night of Ramadan the gates of Hell are locked. The gates of Paradise are opened and they stay open until the end of the month. On that night the devils are chained and thrown to the waves on the oceans so that they cannot bother those who fast. On that night God looks upon humankind. When the Creator looks but once upon someone, He will never punish them.

God forgives in advance the sins one may commit during Ramadan, the moment we start fasting on the first day. And for each day of fasting, a palace of a thousand doors is built for us, and seventy thousand angels pray for our salvation from morning till night. Every night during Ramadan, God Most High speaks to the believers three times and asks: "Is there not anyone who asks, so that I may give them what they ask for? Is there not anyone who repents, so that I may forgive

them? Is there not anyone who wants something from their Lord who is the richest and most generous, who never refuses to give and who is the most merciful and compassionate who forgives all sins?". . .

If the heavens and the Earth were permitted to speak, their first words would have been the good news of God's promise of Paradise to the ones who fast. And if you knew what rewards are promised during this month you would want the whole year to be Ramadan.

A table set out ready to break the fast at Ramadan.

THE FOURTH PILLAR
ZAKAH

At the end of Ramadan, every Muslim household gives one fortieth of its accumulated wealth to the poor. This annual charity is seen as purification of one's wealth. It reminds us that all things come from God, and all things belong to God. We are only the custodians of whatever has come to us. We are expected to be generous with what God has given us.

Fasting causes all Muslims to feel hunger; ideally, this awakens compassion for the poor, which we can act on by giving generously to charity for those less fortunate than ourselves. The sages praise generosity. Ibn Arabi advised: "Spend from what God has given you. Do not fear poverty. God will give you what He has promised, whether you or everyone asks for it or does not ask for it. No one who has been generous has ever perished in destitution." [3]

The Prophet ﷺ taught:

"Give ungrudgingly, lest God be grudging toward you; and do not withhold, lest God withhold from you."

"Jealousy destroys good acts just as fire burns wood; charity consumes sin the same way that water quenches fire."

"True wealth is not abundance in property but a generous heart."

Children sit in class at a Qur'an school, Timbuktu, Mali.

THE FIFTH PILLAR
PILGRIMAGE

All Muslims are required to make a pilgrimage to Makkah if they can afford to do so. The Ka'bah, the shrine in the heart of Makkah, is the holiest site in Islam. It is a stone cube said to have been built by the prophets Abraham and Ishmael عليه السلام, and is the first temple to the One God. Muslims throughout the world perform all their prayers facing this site. The Ka'bah is also known as the *bayt-Allah*, the house of God. Many deeply faithful Muslims from around the world enter into a profound devotional state as they circle the Ka'bah as part of the pilgrimage rituals.

Pilgrimage occurs during a specified week each year and requires a complex set of rigorous observances. Before entering Makkah, all pilgrims have to change into special clothing known as *ihram*. For men this consists of two large pieces of white, unhemmed cloth. One piece is wrapped around the waist and the other goes over the right shoulder. Women wear simple white dresses.

While in the state of *ihram*, pilgrims are to act in some way as though they have already died. They cannot shave, wash themselves, or shampoo their hair. They can stand under running water as if they were standing in the rain, and let it rinse off the worst of the dirt. They cannot even scratch themselves; scratching so that even a few hairs fall out violates *ihram* and voids the pilgrimage. In this state, pilgrims are forbidden to kill anything, even a fly or mosquito. They cannot walk on grass or injure any plant or animal life.

The heart of the pilgrimage is a full day spent in the desert on the plain of Arafat. The mountain of Arafat was the site of the Prophet's ﷺ last sermon, and the whole plain is considered sacred by Muslims.

Years ago, the pilgrimage used to take months. Many would travel on foot or horseback through wilderness and desert to get to Makkah. In addition to the elements, bandits made the trip dangerous. Most Muslims would save up for a lifetime in order to make a single pilgrimage.

In Indonesia today, rural communities will pool their money in order to collect enough for a single couple to make the pilgrimage. No single family could ever earn enough, so each year the community sends the oldest couple who has not yet gone. The whole town will go to Jakarta airport to see off their "representatives." At Hajj time, Jakarta is the most crowded airport in the world.

The pilgrimage is a metaphor for the journey of life. Through God's Messengers we have been given a path to follow throughout our lives. It is described as a difficult, narrow path, and only with God's blessings and guidance can we hope to follow it. The Qur'an teaches that all things come from God and all things return to God, and so the pilgrimage and the journey of life both lead to God's house.

Muslim pilgrims circling the Ka'bah.

The Pilgrimage of a European Muslim

Pilgrims arriving by bus in Saudi Arabia.

The meaning of 'salaam!' (Peace be with you!) seems to be materialized here. Dignity, aesthetics, faith, internationalism. We are particles of a large cosmopolitan unity. In Makkah, racial differences disappear. Only during prayer, when bowing, can I gather from different-colored feet that all races and continents are represented.

"The Ka'bah, prototype of any three-dimensional object, in its utter simplicity, is Islam's answer to the quest for a visual symbol of God's perfection. If He—as Ibn Sina points out—is simplicity in the highest degree, then this empty, undecorated, rough cube symbolizes Him better than any other realizable architectural device. The Ka'bah represents a "still point" and, in as much as it serves as *qiblah* (the global focal point for the direction of prayer), a symbolic anchor of a world religion that knows only too well that God is neither West nor East but beyond the restrictions of time and space.

"On the eve of the all-decisive "Day of Arafat," all pilgrims are tense.... No Arafat, no Hajj. No wonder everyone is a bit nervous. Allah, please, no last-minute hitch! At last, there we all are, more than two million people clad in what looks like their shrouds, anticipating the Day of Judgment, calling out: "*Labbayk Allhumma, labbayk!*" (Here I am, O Allah, at Your disposal!)

"Then, before we know it, we are back in Makkah for the morning prayer, only just making it before sunrise."

"Tired beyond description and happy, also beyond description, we perform our last *tawaf* [circling of the Ka'bah], belatedly realizing that we have become *Hujjaj*, true pilgrims. ...After twenty-six hours on our feet, in this climate, we reach our interim hotel for the next three days in Mina, congratulating each other and asking Allah to accept our pilgrimage." [4]

"Clad in the simple white garb of the pilgrim, we enter the Great Mosque (Masjid al-Haram) and find ourselves facing the Ka'bah at the center of a vast inner courtyard. This is the moment a Muslim hardly dares dream about before it happens. When seeing for the first time architectural or natural monuments with which one is familiar through photographs and films, one is often gravely disappointed. Vision does not meet reality. In this case, however, it is different.

"There is no commercial buzzing around this mosque, nor is there a hot, sacred, or magical atmosphere. Everything is light, dignified, and intensely aesthetic. The large gathering of pilgrims is neither loud nor oppressive. On the contrary, they perform their communal prayers in unison, in a complete silence that protects every person's individuality. Ten thousand pilgrims and visitors silently circumambulate the Ka'bah. The effect is hypnotic. We enjoy the precious feeling of being welcome, fully secure among brethren.

An American Muslim Woman Goes on Pilgrimage

"It was the most difficult thing I've ever done in my whole life. And actually I feel that I was healed of many fears and phobias by doing it—just by walking through fire, so to speak. And I really experienced being ground down to nothing with the exception of the part of me that decided to come because Allah said to. My repeating thoughts, as I sunk lower and lower, were— 'well You asked and I came'—that's all I can say. It wasn't a high experience, it wasn't an ecstatic experience, it was just a grinding down of my personality—all my reactions, all my fears, my judgments, everything was gone, except intention. . . .

"First of all, I was terrified of crowds, and here were two and a half million people jammed into a small space. Not only that, they were people I'd never seen before in my life. It was like the *National Geographic* had just opened and dumped all these people into this place. There were women with henna all over their hands and on their faces. I was just astounded to be in their midst. And of course they were astounded to see me too. Once they knew we were Americans they just went nuts. 'Muslim?' they'd say—'Well, yeah we're here' and they'd go

'O *Alhamdulillah!* [Praise God]' and they'd say prayers and the women would cry. . . .

"I remember the *Labbayk allhumma labbayk* (Here I am Lord, here I am) [chanted continuously by every pilgrim]—hearing that all the time. It was so touching. There was just this murmur of it all the time. . . .

"We often identify an experience that we call spiritual with something that makes us feel good, makes our ego happy. I do believe that it was a very deep experience because of the lack of pleasure. It had nothing to do with pleasure. It had to do with duty . . . it's duty done with pleasure. . . . It is duty done out of love, [but not] . . . to make me feel like a better person, or to get high, or any of that. That was the lesson. As I see it now, really to be 'in the world and not of it' is to accept that the world is not that pleasurable . . . the world tries to capture us in its pleasure and beauty and so forth; but we need to see through that. I don't mean not to appreciate the world—but that there is something beyond, which is more important. It is what we work for, it's what our prayers are for, what our practices are for, what we do Hajj for. It's to honor Allah." [5]

A group of Indonesian women at prayer during pilgrimage.

EXPERIENCE ISLAM

Female members of the family of Akrima Sabri, the Mufti of Jerusalem, pray at home during Ramadan.

from Islamic customs, are not really the same as the experience of worshiping as a Muslim in an Islamic context. You can get a taste of Islam, but to experience the full power and beauty of the Islamic tradition you must be a Muslim.

INTENTION

The Prophet ﷺ taught that the meaning of any action comes from intention. For example, three Muslims decide to make the pilgrimage to Makkah. One wants to go mainly because she wants to fulfill a religious requirement. Another wants to go primarily because he wants the title "*hajji*" and the respect that goes with it. A third wants to go because she yearns to get closer to God.

For every Muslim who decides to make the pilgrimage, there is generally a mixture of all three reasons, plus others as well. Spiritually, it is best to clarify our intentions—to recognize that we have mixed motives and to try and stay focused on our higher aims. People whose religious actions become hijacked by worldly goals may receive worldly compensations for their actions, but they will not receive spiritual benefits. For example, the Prophet ﷺ said, "Some people fast and all they get from it is hunger and thirst."

For a Muslim, every action, such as prayer or fasting, should be preceded by a conscious intention in order for it to count as a religious activity. Many of the practices in this book begin with making intention. The more you experience this process of working consciously with intention, the easier and clearer it becomes.

At the end of each chapter, I have provided practices based on the Islamic tradition, in order to give the reader a firsthand sense of Islam. Often the practices are adapted for non-Muslims, and even practices like prayers and fasting, taken directly

PRAYER

Intention Begin by saying silently, "I make intention to perform two *rakahs* of morning prayer for the pleasure of God."

Ablution Before prayer, we must cleanse ourselves within and without. Outer cleansing is one of the basic requirements of Islamic prayer. We should not seek to enter God's presence without making ourselves clean, and the act of outer cleansing is a metaphor and also an aid to inner cleansing. The following is a simplified form of the Muslim ritual of ablution:

1 Make intention to take abluction; wash your hands three times.
2 Rinse your mouth and nose three times. (To rinse your nose, gently sniff water from your cupped hand.)
3 Wash your face three times.
4 Wash your arms from your wrist to your elbow three times.
5 Run the palm of your wet right hand over your head and over the back of your neck. Then, wash in and around your ears.
6 Wash your feet, up to your ankles, three times.
7 Wash your hands a final time.

• While washing your hands, pray that you will not reach out for anything that is unlawful and that you will open your hands to receive from God and not from the world.
• While washing your mouth, pray that you will continue to praise God and thank God for all you have received, and that you will not misuse your mouth in uttering slander, abuse, or unbelief or in telling lies or swearing.
• While rinsing your nose, pray that God will let you smell the scents of Paradise.
• While washing your face, pray that you will turn your face only toward God, seeking only divine approval.
• While wiping your head, thank God for crowning your head with faith and pray that this crown will never be taken from you.
• While wetting your neck, pray that God will not burden you with the yoke of unbelief and hypocrisy, and while wetting your ears, pray that they will hear only the words of Truth.
• While washing your feet, pray that God will set them firmly on the path of Truth and that you might never stray from this path throughout your life.

Washing the feet as part of pre-prayer ablutions.

Daily Practice The Shariah (Islamic religious law) requires all Muslims to pray five times a day.

When people first embrace Islam as adults, some teachers have allowed them to begin with fewer prayers for a short period of time, as they are learning the form and the Qur'an recitations to go with it.

1 Pray two *rakahs* of morning prayer at dawn. You can begin morning prayer from the time there is the slightest light in the sky until twenty minutes before sunrise. (Most local newspapers list the time of sunrise each day.)
2 Pray three *rakahs* for the evening prayer after the sun has set, while the sky is still light.
3 Pray two *rakahs* of night prayer at least an hour and a half after sunset.

For one month, pray three times a day: mornings, evenings, and nights. Make a clear intention to do this every day for a full month. It may be difficult

A line of Iraqi men performing congregational prayer.

some days, and all kinds of excuses may come to mind, but there is great value in setting this goal and sticking to it.

You can pray in any clean place, except a graveyard or a bathroom. Begin by taking off your shoes.

1 **Standing.** Raise your hands and touch the lobes of your ears with your thumbs, palms forward. Say, "*Allahu akbar*." Then place your hands, right hand over left holding the left wrist, at navel height for men or chest height for women.

Recite *surah* Fatihah (see the English translation on page 13):
Bismillah ir-Rahman ir-Rahim
Al-hamdu lillah-ir Rabbi-l alamin
Ar-Rahman ir-Rahim
Maliki yaum id-din
Iyaka nabudu wa iyaka nastain
Ihdina sirata-l mustaqim
Sirata lathina anamta alaihim
Ghayri-l mahdubi alaihim wa lad-dalin.

Next recite another surah. Begin with *surah* Kawthar, which is very short and easy to learn:
Bismillah-ir Rahman ir-Rahim
Inna atainaka-l kawthar
Fasali li Rabbika wanhar
Inna shaniaka hu al abtar.
(*Behold, We have bestowed upon you goodness in abundance: hence, pray to your Lord [alone], and sacrifice*
[to God alone]
Truly, the ones who hates you is the one cut off
[from all good].)

While you are learning these surahs, recite instead three times "*Allah, Allah, Allah,*" or if you

CHAPTER TWO

THE MESSENGER OF GOD

The Prophet Muhammad  has been chosen by a leading Western historian to head his listing of the world's most influential persons. Not only the founder of one of the world's great religions, he was the only person in history who was extremely successful on both religious and secular levels. Muhammad ﷺ was a philosopher, orator, apostle, legislator, warrior, general, and statesman. He is a role model that all sincere Muslims seek to emulate.

Behold, We have inspired you [O Prophet]
just as We inspired Noah and all the prophets after him—
as We inspired Abraham, and Ishmael, and Isaac,
and Jacob, and their descendants,
including Jesus and Job, and Jonah, and Aaron, and Solomon;
and as We gave unto David a book of divine wisdom;
and as [We inspired other] apostles whom we have
    mentioned to you ere this,
as well as apostles whom We have not mentioned to you;
and as God spoke His word unto Moses:
[We sent all these] apostles as heralds of good tidings and
    as warners,
so that people might have no excuse before God after [the
    coming of] these apostles:
and God is indeed Almighty, Wise. (4:165–146)

God revealed to Muhammad ﷺ the same message that had been revealed to Abraham, Moses, and Jesus عليه السلام. Muhammad ﷺ was an inspiring religious teacher, a visionary social reformer, a brilliant civic and national leader, a gifted general, and a skilled politician. He was a man of great gentleness, generosity, compassion, and piety. The life of Muhammad ﷺ has been well documented. We know how he lived at home, how he prayed, how he taught, and how he ruled. Muslims do not regard Muhammad ﷺ as God, or as a divine figure. However, he is considered insan al-kamil, a perfect human being.

THE PROPHET ﷺ SAID, "O PEOPLE, TURN TO GOD IN REPENTANCE, AND SEEK FORGIVENESS OF GOD. INDEED, I REPENT A HUNDRED TIMES A DAY."

EARLY LIFE

Muhammad ﷺ was born in the year 570 C.E.[1] His father died before he was born and his mother died when he was still a child. Shortly after he was born, Muhammad ﷺ was given to Bedouin foster parents. This was a common practice among city Arabs, who believed the desert was healthier than the city and the nomadic life of the Bedouin developed character and fortitude.

When he was six, Muhammad's ﷺ mother died, and he went to live with his grandfather. Two years later his grandfather died, and Muhammad ﷺ joined the household of his uncle, Abu Talib. His uncle was chief of the Hashim clan, one of the clans of the powerful Quraish, the tribe that dominated Makkah. Abu Talib was poor but well respected in Makkah. Makkah was a wealthy and powerful city. It was an oasis in the desert, a major stop for desert caravans, and the chief trading center in Arabia. Travelers from all over Arabia and beyond came to Makkah.

As a young man, Muhammad ﷺ was known for his honor and integrity. He was nicknamed al-amin, the reliable, by those who knew him. Muhammad ﷺ grew up to be an able, honorable young man. He was of average height, and his hair and beard were thick and wavy. He had a striking, luminous expression and a noble character. Muhammad ﷺ became a merchant and trader and led caravans to Syria and Mesopotamia. This was a demanding and sometimes dangerous job, requiring intelligence, patience, courage, and leadership. He was hired for a trading journey by Khadijah, a well-to-do widow and a successful merchant. Khadijah came to know Muhammad ﷺ and to admire his character, and she proposed marriage to him. They married and raised a family. They had two sons, who died in infancy, and four daughters. Throughout their marriage Khadijah was

Moorish men recite the life of Muhammad.

one of Muhammad's ﷺ strongest supporters, and they were deeply in love with each other.

Muhammad ﷺ was always heavily interested in religious and spiritual matters. Although he and Khadijah were relatively wealthy, they gave most of their income to the poor and led a simple, frugal life. Muhammad ﷺ often spent time in long vigils and prayers in secluded caves in the mountains surrounding Makkah.

In 610, when he was 40, Muhammad ﷺ went into seclusion in a cave on nearby Mount Hira. While sitting in contemplation, the archangel Gabriel appeared to him. This awesome angelic Prescence commanded, "Iqraa" ("Read" or "recite"). Muhammad ﷺ was unlettered and he replied, "I cannot read." The angel seized him and embraced him so hard all the strength went out of him. Gabriel repeated, "Recite!" and again Muhammad ﷺ replied, "I cannot." Gabriel crushed Muhammad ﷺ to himself a second time and repeated once

more, "Recite!" Muhammad ﷺ again replied, "I cannot read." Gabriel embraced Muhammad ﷺ a third time and then imparted the first revelation of the Qur'an:

> Read in the name of your Sustainer,
> who has created—
> Created humanity out of a germ cell!
> Read—for your Lord
> is the Most Generous One
> Who has taught [the use of] the Pen,
> taught humanity what they did not know! (96:1–5)

"THOSE WHO GO OUT IN SEARCH OF KNOWLEDGE ARE ON THE PATH OF GOD UNTIL THEY RETURN." MUHAMMAD ﷺ

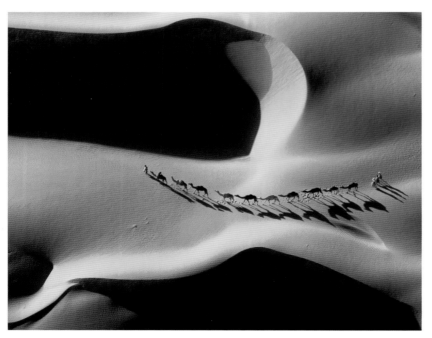

A caravan of camels being led across the desert in Mauritania.

of God. Because of her faith in Muhammad ﷺ, Khadijah accepted the message he received and became the first Muslim.

The revelations continued, and Muhammad ﷺ had to struggle to understand them. Some revelations were more like visions than words. For almost two years, he strove alone, still unsure if he was deluded or not. Finally, Muhammad ﷺ began to share with others what had been revealed to him.

"AVOID THREE QUALITIES: JEALOUSY, GREED, AND REGRET." MUHAMMAD ﷺ

Muhammad ﷺ realized that he was commanded to "read," to receive and understand, God's Message and teach it to humanity. He returned home deeply shaken by his experience. He was shivering, in a state of shock. Khadijah held him and covered him with a blanket. She asked him what had happened, and he told her the story and added he was not sure if he had really encountered an angel or a *jinn* (a supernatural spirit), or a figment of his imagination.

Khadijah consulted her cousin, a devout Christian Arab, who confirmed her belief that her husband was destined to be a prophet. Khadijah assured Muhammad ﷺ that she believed in him. She was sure he had really met an angel. She knew that he had the impeccable character of a prophet and believed that he was to become a great prophet

His message was simple. His teachings about God were basically the same as the teachings of the Jews and Christians. Muhammad ﷺ stressed social equality and social justice. He taught that the wealthy were obliged to help the poor and that all men and women were equal before God. He guided his followers to behave with honesty, equity, and compassion for others.

Many of the members of wealthier and more powerful clans became jealous. They refused to believe that an obscure, unlettered orphan was a prophet. They were sure that they were more worthy of prophethood. A small community of believers developed. Many were poor or slaves. As the Muslim community grew, the envy of the more powerful turned to hatred and persecution. More and more people began to follow Muhammad ﷺ, and his following grew to some 70 families.

However, when Muhammad ﷺ taught that people were to worship God alone and to abandon their worship of the old tribal gods, many of his

"THE BEST PEOPLE ARE THOSE WHO ARE MOST USEFUL TO OTHERS." MUHAMMAD ﷺ

followers left. The wealthy and powerful became incensed when he warned that on the Day of Judgment each individual would be judged on his or her merit, and wealth and position would be of no help. His teachings split the city of Makkah. It became dangerous for the poor and less influential Muslims. Many were ridiculed or beaten for their beliefs. Some of the Muslim slaves were tortured by their owners.

The verses of the Qur'an began to circulate within and also beyond Makkah. Many became Muslims because of the power and beauty of the Qur'an. The Qur'an created a new literary form, a masterpiece of Arabic poetry and prose. These revelations inspired listeners, as great art always does. Umar, one of the more powerful men of Makkah, was passionately opposed to Muhammad's teaching and vowed to wipe out Islam. However, when he first heard the words of the Qur'an, he was overcome by their eloquence. Later, he said, "When I heard the Qur'an my heart was softened and I wept, and Islam entered into me." Umar became one of the closeset companions of the Prophet ﷺ, a great defender of Islam, and the second caliph after the passing away of the Prophet ﷺ.

The powerful Makkan clans responded to the spread of Islam in about 616 C.E. with a boycott of those clans that supported Muhammad and his followers. No one could marry or trade with boycotted clan members, or sell them food. The persecuted clan members were expelled from the city to a barren valley a few miles away. The ban lasted for over two years and created food shortages and tremendous hardships for the Muslims and their relatives and supporters.

Muhammad ﷺ asked the Christian king of Abyssinia to take in the most vulnerable Muslims, and the king agreed. About 83 Muslims and their households left Makkah for Abyssinia.

In about 619 C.E., after the ban was lifted, both Khadijah and Muhammad's uncle Abu Talib passed away. The new chief of Muhammad's clan was one of his worst enemies, and Muhammad ﷺ and his followers became much more vulnerable to the persecutions of his adversaries.

When things looked darkest, Muhammad ﷺ had his greatest mystical experience, known as the Lailat ul-miraj, or the Night Journey. He was awakened by the archangel Gabriel. Accompanied by Gabriel, Muhammand ﷺ was carried on a heavenly steed to ride to Jerusalem. Jerusalem is the location of the Prophet Solomon's عليه السلام temple and the place where Jesus عليه السلام taught. At first, the Muslims prayed in the direction of Jerusalem and not toward the Ka'bah in Makkah.

In Jerusalem Muhammad ﷺ met with the spirits of Abraham, Moses, Jesus, and many other great prophets عليه السلام. They all prayed together, with Muhammad ﷺ leading the prayer. Then Gabriel took Muhammad ﷺ, and they ascended through the seven heavens. Finally, Muhammad ﷺ ascended alone to the Throne of God, and there he conversed directly with God.

Studying the Qur'an at night by lamplight.

"WORSHIP GOD AS IF YOU SEE HIM, AND REMEMBER THAT EVEN IF YOU DO NOT SEE GOD, GOD STILL SEES YOU." MUHAMMAD ﷺ

CONTINUED PERSECUTION

Makkan persecution continued, and even Muhammad ﷺ was no longer safe. He had to do something to save his followers and himself. In 620 C.E. Muhammad ﷺ met with a group of six

> "THOSE WHO DO NOT EXPRESS THEIR GRATITUDE TO PEOPLE WILL NEVER BE ABLE TO BE GRATEFUL TO GOD." MUHAMMAD ﷺ

pilgrims from the city of Yathrib. He explained Islam to them, and they accepted it. Then, Muhammad ﷺ sent one of his most able followers to Yathrib to teach the Qur'an and the principles of Islam.

Two years later a group of over 70 pilgrims came from Yathrib and secretly met with Muhammad ﷺ and accepted Islam. The tribes that had settled in Yathrib were fighting constantly, raiding each other's territory or seeking to avenge damage done by a rival tribe. The visitors

represented two of the major tribes of Yathrib and they invited Muhammad ﷺ to rule their strife-torn city. He agreed and then instructed his followers to leave for Yathrib. They left quietly in small groups. It was the year 622 C.E., and Muhammad ﷺ had been teaching Islam in Makkah for 12 years.

The year of emigration to Yathrib became the start of the Muslim calendar. It was a life-changing decision for the early Muslims. In Arabia, the tribe was sacred. To leave your blood relatives and join another community was unheard of, even blasphemous. The Quraish were infuriated over the exodus of the Muslims and vowed to exterminate the small emigrant community.

The Makkans decided to destroy Islam by murdering Muhammad ﷺ. Young men from each clan were to sneak into his house at night and stab him together. This way Muhammad's clan would be unable to take revenge on any single group.

When Muhammad ﷺ found out about the plot, he slipped out of town with Abu Bakr, one of his closest friends and most devoted followers. They hid in a cave for three days while the Makkans sent warriors scouring the desert. Then, the two men set out in the opposite direction of Yathrib and circled

Arabia and the surrounding areas at the time of Muhammad, about 610 C.E.

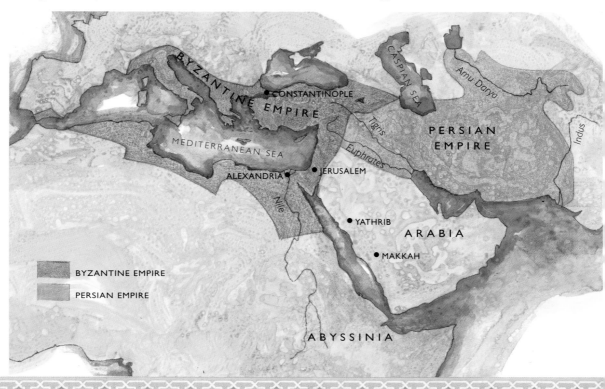

BYZANTINE EMPIRE

PERSIAN EMPIRE

back, eluding the searchers. They finally reached Yathrib, which soon became known as Madinah.

The Muslim immigrants had come with only the few belongings they could carry, and so Muhammad ﷺ asked the Muslims of Madinah to "adopt" the immigrants. Each immigrant family was taken in by a Madinah family, who shared their homes and food with the newcomers.

A NEW SOCIAL STRUCTURE

Muhammad ﷺ wrote a city charter guaranteeing the rights of all residents, and he sent treaties of friendship to neighboring tribes and cities. Bolstered by continuing revelations, he developed a new legal code, and new moral and ethical standards for the growing Muslim community. Muhammad ﷺ founded a radically new social structure for Arabia. He became head of a collection of tribal groups bound together by shared beliefs, not by blood kinship.

No one was forced to convert to Islam. The Qur'an clearly states, "There shall be no coercion in matters of faith" (2:256). Jews and Christians were honored as "People of the Book." Muhammad ﷺ never felt they had to embrace Islam as they had their own divinely revealed scriptures and laws to follow.

Three times in the next five years (624–629 C.E.), Makkah sent invading forces to destroy Islam. The Muslims were outnumbered in each battle, but each time managed to defeat the invaders. Before the battle of Badr, Makkah assembled a thousand warriors, well equipped with horses, camels, weapons, and armor. Muhammad ﷺ had a force of only 313 poorly equipped followers. (The Muslim warriors were accompanied by their wives and daughters who tended the wounded on the battlefield. The women even took an active part in the battles on occasion.)

"THERE ARE AS MANY WAYS TO GOD AS THERE ARE SOULS." MUHAMMAD ﷺ

Muhammad ﷺ decided to confront the Makkan army at the oasis of Badr. The Muslims got there first and took control of the wells. Even though they were tired and thirsty from their long desert journey, the Makkans saw that they outnumbered the Muslims and engaged them in battle. They were routed, losing several leaders. Almost one hundred men were killed or taken prisoner, while the Muslims had minimal casualties.

At the battle of Uhud, Makkah assembled an army of three thousand warriors to attack the Muslims. Muhammad ﷺ managed to gather one thousand men and proceeded to Mount Uhud, a small mountain just outside Madinah. The day before the battle, one of the Madinah leaders deserted with three hundred of his men, leaving only seven hundred men to fight three thousand.

Muhammad ﷺ formed his men in close ranks and placed fifty archers on a side hill to prevent the enemy cavalry from sweeping around to attack from the rear. The enemy charged, and the Muslim soldiers held. The Muslims countercharged, and the enemy began to retreat in confusion. The archers left their position on the hill to join in the battle, and the Makkan cavalry raced around Mount Uhud and attacked the Muslims from behind.

The Muslims were forced to retreat, losing their chance of a stunning victory against great odds. Muhammad ﷺ tried to stop the retreat but was knocked unconscious by a blow to the head. Muslim women surrounded him and protected him from the enemy. The Makkan army withdrew, thinking that Muhammad ﷺ was dead and Islam destroyed.

Before the third battle, Makkah made alliances with tribes throughout Arabia and assembled an army of of over ten thousand to attack Madinah. Madinah was surrounded on three sides by cliffs and plains of volcanic rock. A Persian Muslim, Salman al-Farsi, had studied military tactics and strategy. He advised strengthening the walls of Madinah and building a deep trench or moat along the exposed front section of the city. Every family was responsible for a different section of the trench, and it took the concerted efforts of all the Muslims to get it finished in time.

The Makkan army tried to breach the trench for almost a month. Their cavalry was unable to breach the trench, and their attacks on foot were beaten back each time by the Madinah archers, firing down from a wall made up of the earth taken from the trench.

The Makkan army was not prepared for a siege. Desert warfare was usually a matter of sudden hit-and-run raids and cavalry charges. They were out of provisions, and the men and horses were hungry. A storm broke out, and one of the tribal leaders left along with his warriors. The other Bedouin then left as well, and the Makkans had to retreat. The siege was lifted.

Although these early battles give the impression that Islam is a militant, conflict-loving religion, the opposite is true. The Qur'an teaches that war is a catastrophe to be avoided if at all possible. Islam urges people to do everything possible to seek peace and end conflict.

"Shall I tell you about the people of Paradise? They include every one of those who are powerless and slighted, yet who certainly fulfill any oath to God they make. Shall I tell you about the people of hell? They include everyone who is violent, recalcitrant, and arrogant." Muhammad ﷺ 2

Far right: Iraqi Shiite woman with child.

After these victories, the Muslims gained great status throughout Arabia. Many tribes began converting to Islam, and Muslim strength began to

"ACTIONS ARE BASED ON INTENTIONS." MUHAMMAD ﷺ

rival that of Makkah. The following year, 629 C.E., Muhammad ﷺ initiated an unprecedented peace offensive during the pilgrimage season. He journeyed to Makkah with over one thousand virtually unarmed Muslims wearing the traditional white robes of the pilgrims. Makkah sent a troop of two hundred cavalry to stop the Muslims, but the Muslims took a footpath through the mountains and came to the edge of the city, where violence was forbidden by ancient custom.

The Makkans were afraid to let the Muslims into the city, but they knew that they could not simply forbid over a thousand pilgrims who were scrupulously observing the ancient Arab pilgrimage rituals. Their reputation would have suffered throughout Arabia. Makkah sent a delegation to Muhammad ﷺ and worked out the treaty of Hudaybiyyah. This was a ten-year peace treaty between Makkah and Madinah. It also allowed the Muslims to make pilgrimages to Makkah. However, many Muslims wanted to continue their fight against Makkah and felt the treaty was shameful.

The treaty of Hudaybiyyah impressed many of the Bedouin tribes and the numbers of Muslims continued to increase. However, the treaty was broken when a tribe allied to Makkah attacked a tribe allied to Madinah. In 630 C.E. Muhammad ﷺ brought an army of ten thousand Muslims to

Makkah. They camped in the mountains surrounding the city, and Muhammad ﷺ ordered his soldiers to make several campfires for each group, so his army seemed larger.

Makkah surrendered, and the next day, the Muslims entered the city without shedding a drop of blood. Muhammad ﷺ pardoned those who had tortured him and his followers for so many years. Then he cleared out all the idols from the Ka'bah. None of the Makkans were forced to embrace Islam. After a few weeks, Muhammad ﷺ returned to Madinah, which was to remain the center of the growing Islamic state.

In 632 C.E., when he was almost 63 years of age, Muhammad ﷺ made a final pilgrimage to Makkah. He delivered a famous talk on Mount Arafat, known as his Last Sermon. When Muhammad ﷺ returned to Madinah, he fell ill and passed away several weeks later.

A MOTHER'S LOVE

One day, a woman came to the Prophet ﷺ, deeply upset that her son was not of good character, convinced that he was going to go to hell when he died. The Prophet ﷺ, along with several of his companions, went with her to her house. He ordered some of the companions to bring rope and tie up the son. Others he had bring wood and make a roaring fire in the mother's kitchen stove.

His companions brought the bound son into the kitchen. The Prophet ﷺ told the mother that he would save her son from the eternal fires of hell by burning him right now. That way the son would atone for his sins in this world and not in the next. The mother cried and screamed and began to fight with the companions in order to free her son.

The Prophet ﷺ told her to stop. "Because of your love for him, you would never let your son be put in the fire in spite of whatever he has done wrong. God loves each of us a thousand times more than the love a mother has for her child. Just as you would never let your son be put in the fire, neither will God."

HADITH: THE TRADITIONS OF THE PROPHET ﷺ

Illuminated section of the Qur'an.

The example of the Prophet ﷺ became known as the *sunnah*, his customs. Individual sayings are called *hadith*. Hundreds of thousands of *hadith* were collected during and immediately after the Prophet's ﷺ lifetime. His widow Aishah ﷻ and a few close companions contributed over two thousand *hadith* apiece. Several collections of *hadith* are considered the most authoritative. The *hadith* collectors would examine the evidence for each *hadith*. Along with the text of the saying, each *hadith* contains a chain of recorders and transmitters. If anyone in that chain was suspected of poor character or untruth, the hadith would be discarded. In the *hadith qudsi*, God spoke directly through Muhammad ﷺ, in an extra-Qur'anic revelation.

MUHAMMAD ﷺ AND THE KITTEN

One day Muhammad ﷺ was sitting in the shade under a tree. A kitten came and curled up on his cloak and went to sleep. When the time came for him to go, Muhammad ﷺ took his knife and cut away part of his cloak so as not to disturb the sleeping kitten.

Far right: Muslim men praying at a mosque in Bhagdad, Iraq.

A DESCRIPTION OF THE PROPHET ﷺ

The following describes the Prophet Muhammad ﷺ as seen through the eyes of one who loved him deeply, his son-in-law and the fourth caliph Ali ﷻ. It gives us a sense of the Prophet's ﷺ charisma, his enormous appeal to those who followed his teachings and his example.

"He was neither tall and lanky nor short and stocky, but of medium height. His hair was neither crisply curled nor straight but moderately wavy. He was not overweight, and his face was not plump. He had a round face. His complexion was white tinged with reddishness. He had big black eyes with long lashes. His bones were heavy and his shoulders broad. He had soft skin, with fine hair covering the line from mid-chest to navel. The palms of his hands and the soles of his feet were firmly padded. He walked with a firm gait, as if striding downhill. On his back between his shoulders lay the Seal of Prophethood, for he was the last of the prophets.

"He was the most generous of men in feeling, the most truthful in speech, the gentlest in disposition, and the noblest in lineage. At first encounter people were awestruck by him, but on closer acquaintance they would come to love him. One who sought to describe him could only say, 'Neither before him nor after him did I ever see the like of him'".

EXCERPTS FROM THE PROPHET'S ﷺ LAST SERMON

O People, listen well to what I say. I do not know whether, after this year, I shall ever meet you here again. Listen to what I am saying to you carefully and take these words to those who could not be present here today, and it may be that someone who hears it from you will understand it and keep it better than those listening here and now.

O People, just as you regard this month, this day, this city as sacred, so regard the life and property of every Muslim as a sacred trust. Return the goods entrusted to you to

their rightful owners. Hurt no one so that no one may hurt you. Remember that you will indeed meet your Lord, and that God will indeed reckon your deeds. God has forbidden you to take usury; therefore all interest obligation shall henceforth be waived.

Beware of Satan, for the safety of your religion. He has lost hope that he will ever be able to lead you astray in big things, so beware of following him in small things.

O People, listen to me in earnest, worship God, say your five daily prayers, fast during the month of Ramadan, and give your wealth in zakah. Perform Hajj if you

can afford to. All humankind is from Adam and Eve; an Arab has no superiority over a non-Arab nor has a non-Arab any superiority over an Arab; also, a white has no superiority over a black nor has a black any superiority over a white except through piety and good action. Learn that every Muslim is a brother to every other Muslim and that the Muslims constitute one brotherhood. Nothing shall be legitimate to a Muslim that belongs to a fellow Muslim unless it was given freely and willingly. Do not therefore, do injustice to yourselves.

Remember, one day you will appear before God and answer for your deeds. So beware, do not stray from the path of righteousness after I am gone.

O People, no prophet or apostle will come after me and no new faith will be born. Reason well, therefore, O People, and understand my words, which I convey to you. I leave behind me two things, the Qur'an and my example, the sunnah, and if you follow these you will never go astray.

All those who listen to me shall pass on my words to others and those to others again; and may the last ones understand my word better than those who listen to me directly. Be my witness O God that I have conveyed your message to your people.[3]

A CHRONOLOGY OF THE LIFE OF THE PROPHET ﷺ

570 C.E. The Prophet Muhammad ﷺ is born.

610 C.E. Muhammad ﷺ receives the first revelations of the Qur'an.

612 C.E. Muhammad ﷺ begins to teach publicly.

c.615 C.E. The Muslim community is persecuted by the rich and powerful in Makkah.

622 Hijrah—Seventy Muslim families migrate to Yathrib (Madinah) followed by Muhammad ﷺ.

624 C.E. The Battle of Badr—Muslims win a dramatic victory over Makkan forces.

625 C.E. The Battle of Uhud—Muslim forces are routed after an initial victory.

627 C.E. The Battle of the Trench—Muslims hold off and defeat a besieging Makkan army.

628 C.E. Peace treaty is signed between Makkah and Madinah.

630 C.E. Makkah violates the peace treaty. Muhammad ﷺ and his army enter Makkah unopposed.

632 C.E. Death of the Prophet Muhammad ﷺ.

Time to reflect at the end of the day.

A Western Muslim's Appreciation of the Prophet ﷺ

Murad Hoffman is a German diplomat who embraced Islam in mid-career. He was Information Director of NATO and also German ambassador to Algeria and Morocco. Leaving aside what a propensity to see miracles and a tendency toward political partisanship may have contributed, Muhammad ﷺ emerges from [historical] sources as a statesman-like personality of great charisma, willpower, and tactical prowess.

The period between his emigration to Madinah and his peaceful conquest of Makkah one decade later, shows him to be a strategist to be mentioned in the same breath as the nineteenth-century Prussian general Carl von Clausewitz. Muhammad ﷺ had already consciously applied economic and psychological warfare and used arms control negotiations as an instrument of foreign policy. The armistice he accepted at Hudaybiyah—to the consternation of his entourage—was a diplomatic coup of the first order, and the Makkans soon realized that they had signed themselves into future capitulation. Equally extraordinary was the constitution of Madinah, dictated by Muhammad ﷺ as a federative treaty between the Muslim and Jewish communities.

If one also takes into account Muhammad's ﷺ success in trade and commerce, his wisdom as judge and arbitrator, and the stylistic power and beauty of his pronouncements, one is at a loss to explain how an uneducated, illiterate, "backward" Arab could possess such qualities.

There is something uncanny about it.

There is something divine about it.[4]

duty of immediately writing down the revelations of the Qur'an. After each revelation, they read back to him for his approval what they had written. This group became the teachers and compilers of the Qur'an during the Prophet's ﷺ lifetime and after his death.

When receiving revelation, sometimes Muhammad ﷺ would shiver or break out in a cold sweat, even in the desert heat. When a revelation came while he was sitting on his camel, his camel buckled to its knees under the weight of the divine words. The Qur'an teaches:

> Had We sent down
> this Qur'an on a mountain,
> truly, you would have seen
> it humble itself and split asunder
> for fear of God. (59:21)

Before he passed away, Muhammad ﷺ prescribed the ordering of the surahs, or chapters, of the Qur'an. The ordering is not historical; for example, many of the earlier, short Makkan surahs are placed at the end. The group of Muhammad's ﷺ scribes collected all the written and memorized versions of Qur'anic revelations. Minor discrepancies among versions were resolved by those who were actually present while the Qur'an was revealed, and by those who had already memorized all or most of the Qur'an. Twenty years after the passing away of the Prophet ﷺ, an official text was agreed on and copies were placed in every Muslim city. The Qur'an has remained unaltered for 14 centuries, which is itself a minor miracle.

As Islam spread, the Qur'an and the Arabic language and culture spread with it. Arabic has influenced many other languages, and Arabic script is used for writing languages including Persian, Urdu, Ottoman Turkish, Pashto, Kashmiri, Sindi, and Malay.

The Qur'an is made up of 114 surahs and 6,666 ayahs or verses. The shortest surah has only three ayahs, and the longest is 286 ayahs. An ayah is

"OH PEOPLE, ALL MY INSTRUCTIONS ARE ACCORDING TO THE QUR'AN, AND IF YOU COME ACROSS ANYTHING THAT DOES NOT AGREE WITH THE QUR'AN, IT IS NOT MY WORD." MUHAMMAD ﷺ [2]

literally a "sign," and so each verse of the Qur'an is a sign of God. Every surah, except the ninth, begins with the phrase *Bismillah ar-rahman ar-rahim*, "In the Name of God, Most Gracious, Most Merciful." This is the most frequently uttered phrase in the world, used by devout Muslims before beginning any Qur'anic recitation and also before beginning any significant activity.

The Qur'an provides an explicit moral and legal code, but it is also the transcendent Divine Word, the meaning of which is inexhaustible. Some scholars teach that in essence the Qur'an is written in the language of God, although it has the outer form of Arabic. The Qur'an applies to daily life and links it to the transcendent. The Qur'an includes ethical and religious precepts, prohibitions of unlawful acts, commandments of lawful activities, promise of reward for the pious, and threats of punishment for the wrongdoers. It also contains parables, metaphors, and stories of the old prophets ﷺ. In addition, the Qur'an explains the religious obligations of prayer, fasting, charity, and pilgrimage to Makkah.

There are two dimensions to Qur'anic teachings—inner and outer. The outer dimension includes the concrete commandments, prohibitions, and teachings. The inner, esoteric dimension refers to the timeless, transcendent level of meaning. Every ayah contains both of these dimensions and multiple levels of meaning.

"What initially strikes the reader confronted for the first time with a text of this kind is the sheer abundance of subjects discussed: the Creation, astronomy, the explanation of certain matters concerning the Earth, the animal and vegetable kingdoms, and human reproduction. Whereas monumental errors are to be found in the Bible, I could not find a single error in the Qur'an. I had to stop and ask myself: if a man was the author of the Qur'an, how could he have written facts in the seventh century C.E. that today are shown to be in keeping with modern scientific knowledge? There was absolutely no doubt about it: the text of the Qur'an we have today is most definitely a text of that period, if I may be allowed to put it in these terms. . . ."

What human explanation can there be to this observation? In my opinion, there is no explanation; there is no special reason why an inhabitant of the Arabian Peninsula should, at a time when King Dagobert I was reigning in France (629–39 C.E.), have had scientific knowledge on certain subjects that was ten centuries ahead of our own." [3]

COMMENTARIES ON THE QUR'AN

Muslim scholars have developed the science of Qur'anic commentary, the interpretation and explanation of the text of the Qur'an. Throughout Islamic history, many of the finest Muslim scholars devoted themselves to commentary on the Qur'an.

THE PROPHET ﷺ ON THE IMPORTANCE OF KNOWLEDGE

Acquire knowledge, for surely it leads to consciousness of God. Seeking it is an act of worship; studying it is praising God; seeking it is jihad [struggle to follow in the way of God]; teaching it to whomever doesn't know it is an act of charity; and giving it to one's people draws one closer to them.

Knowledge points to the permissible and the prohibited, and it is a shining light pointing the way to Paradise. It comforts the lonely, befriends the estranged, and talks to you in seclusion. It is a guide through prosperity and adversity.

With knowledge, God raises people to high stations, making them leaders in goodness whose steps are traced. Their example is emulated, their opinion followed. The angels like to sit with the people of knowledge, surrounding them with their wings, and everything dry or wet—fish of the sea and animals on land—will ask God to forgive them.

For knowledge gives life to the heart in the midst of ignorance, and illumines vision in the darkness. With knowledge, God's servants become the elite and reach the highest degrees in this life and in the hereafter.

Contemplation with knowledge is equivalent to fasting; spending time to study is equivalent to standing at night in prayer. Knowledge precedes action and action always follows it. [4]

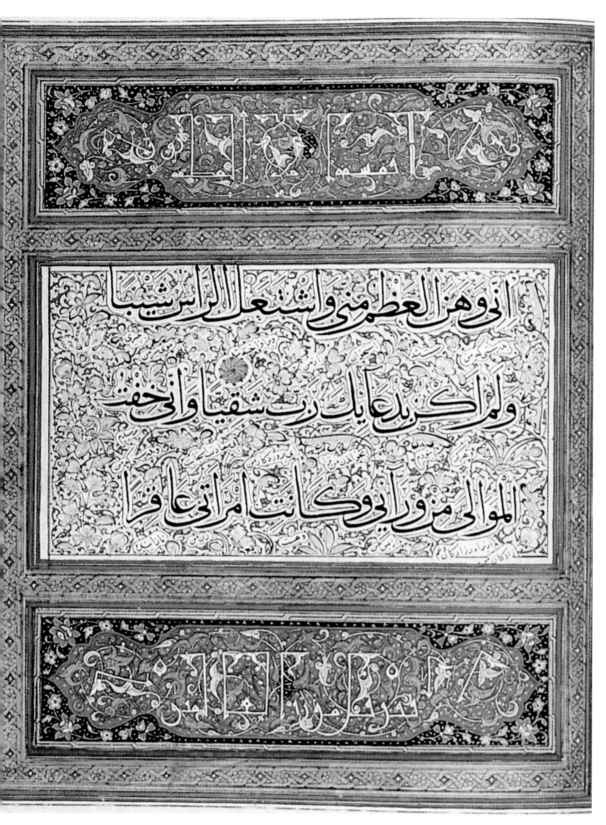

A Qur'anic manuscript
written about 1400
C.E. in the style which
prevailed in Persia and
Iraq showing the first
verses from the
surah Maryam.

Every surah of the Qur'an, save one, begins with the holy phrase, Bismillah ar-Rahman ar-Rahim.

SURAH FATIHAH

The *Fatihah* is one of the early surahs, revealed in Makkah. It soon became a required part of every prayer. The *Fatihah* is said to possess deep mysteries and also healing power.

Right: A page from the Qur'an showing the surah Fatihah.

Bismillah ar-Rahman ar-Rahim
(In the Name of God, Most Gracious, Most Merciful)
All praise is due to God alone, the Sustainer of all
        the Worlds.
Most Gracious, Most Merciful,
Lord of the Day of Judgment.
You alone do we worship, and to You alone do we
        turn for help.
Guide us along the straight path—
The path of those whom you have blessed, not of those
        who have been condemned [by You], nor of those
        who go astray. (1:1–7)

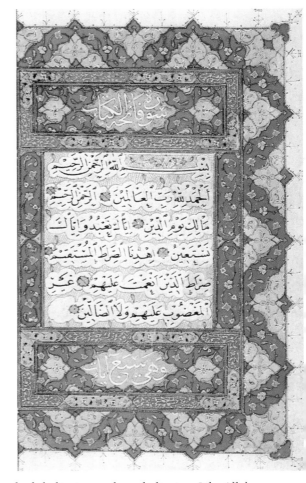

The opening line, the *Bismillah ar-Rahman ar-Rahim*, contains three Divine Names. Allah is the Greatest Name and contains all the other Attributes of God. It is also the sign of the Divine Essence. It refers to God as the cause of existence, and, as such, Allah does not in any way resemble Creation. Nothing else can assume this name or is allowed to share it in any way.

As ar-Rahman, God wills mercy and good for all Creation at all times. God's grace pours upon all Creation, without distinction between good and bad, believing and nonbelieving. Like Allah, ar-Rahman is a proper name of God and cannot be attributed to others.

As ar-Rahim, God is the source of infinite mercy and rewards those who use divine bounties for good. This aspect of Divine Mercy is directed toward those who use their will in accordance with God's Will and who act to please God.

As mentioned in Chapter 1, commentators have pointed out that *surah Fatihah* has three parts. In the first part, the reciters praise God, and through this act of praise they connect themselves to God. In the second part, the reciters affirm that their goal is to worship God alone and to rely on God alone. In the third part, the worshipers ask for divine help, for the greatest of gifts, which is God's guidance along the path of Truth. In the first part of the surah, each verse of praise brings a response from God.

In a *hadith qudsi*, God declares, "When a servant of Mine says, 'All praise is due to God alone,' I respond, 'My servant has praised Me.' When a servant says, 'Most Gracious, Most Merciful,' I say, 'My servant has exalted Me.' And when my servant recites, 'Lord of the Day of Judgment,' I acknowledge, 'My servant has glorified Me.'" The term "Lord of the Day of Judgment" also reminds us that all things come from God and all things will eventually return to God.

Those who recite this surah hope to come closer to God. When close to God, the believer sees no one but God, and knows nothing else is worthy of worship. The believer realizes that nothing and no one else but God has the power or strength to accomplish anything. In reciting that we worship God alone and only seek help from God, we express the hope that these words will become true for us. It also refers to God's Mercy both here and in the hereafter.

In the third part of the surah, we ask God to guide us on the straight path, the path of the prophets, the saints, the friends of God. Without God we can do nothing. We seek the blessing of God's guidance, for without that guidance we are lost. Those who have incurred God's condemnation are those who received guidance and who have understood God's message, but have rejected it. Those who have gone astray are those who have not received God's message at all, or who received only an incomplete or distorted version of the Truth.

This final verse can also be understood as referring to each of us. There is the part of us that rejects truth or distorts religious teachings and practices because of the distortions of our egos and our attachments to material gains and pleasures.

Boys and girls studying the Qur'an in a traditional school, or madrasa.

SURAH BAQARA

The following verses are from the beginning of the second surah of the Qur'an, which is also the longest:

Below: The Hussein Mosque, Kerbala. Mosques are traditionally decorated with calligraphy from the Qur'an.

Alif, Lam, Mim
This is the Book in which there is no doubt,
Guidance for all the God-fearing
who believe in the Unseen, beyond human perception,
and are constant in prayer,
and who spend out of what We provide for them
as sustenance,
and who believe in that which has been bestowed from on high upon you
[O Prophet],
as well as in that which was bestowed before your time.
For it is they who in their innermost being are certain of the life to come!
It is they who follow the guidance from their sustainer
And it is they, they who shall attain a happy state.
(2:1–5)

This surah begins with three unconnected Arabic letters, and many commentaries have provided different interpretations of their meaning. There are 29 surahs that begin with from two to five unconnected letters. Many commentators assert that the unconnected letters belong to the part of the Qur'an that is hidden and therefore cannot be understood or interpreted by human beings. They are a reminder of the fundamental mystery of divine revelation, and there is no universal agreement as to their meaning.

Verse two reminds us that the Qur'an is truly God's Book; therefore, it contains only Truth. It is not guidance for everyone, however. The Qur'an is only a guide for those who are ready to receive it. These are the "God-fearing," those who know that God is always present and therefore constantly watch their speech and actions in order to avoid saying or doing anything that might displease God. They are not afraid of God's punishment so much as they are afraid they might separate themselves from God. Instead of God-fearing they might be called the God-conscious.

The God-conscious believe that beyond the material reality that surrounds us there is a deeper reality, a reality that cannot be perceived by our five

senses. Those materialists who believe only in material reality cannot believe in God, Who is unseen, and therefore the Qur'an remains a closed book for them.

The God-conscious of all religions pray regularly. The God-conscious are also generous in charity because they know that whatever has come to them has come from God. Here the Qur'an reminds us that faith includes inner expression, which is prayer, as well as outer expression, which is generosity.

The believers know that God has sent down the Truth to us through all the great prophets, including Muhammad ﷺ, and the revelations sent to each prophet are all essentially the same. Those who fit these criteria are people whose hearts and minds are open to the Truth and who sincerely try to follow the Truth. The capacity to understand and to follow God's guidance is itself a great gift from God.

SURAH IKHLAS

This short surah is one of the most important in the Qur'an. It is said to contain one third of the wisdom of the Qur'an.

> *Say: He is God.*
> *The One and Only.*
> *God is the Satisfier of all needs,*
> *neither born, nor giving birth,*
> *and there is none like God*
> *Who is Unique.* (112:1–4)

This surah beautifully expresses God's unity and uniqueness. God is One, the essence and source of Unity. God is Self-Sufficient, the One who satisfies all needs—all are in need of God, yet God needs nothing. Everything in Creation is in need. For example, everything needs the right environment

God's Mercy can be seen in the rain, which brings life to seemingly dead soil.

in order to survive. If it is too hot, material things will melt or burn. Without oxygen or nourishment, living things will die. Only God remains unaffected by any changes in Creation.

All things in Creation are born or generated from something else, and all things give rise to other things. For example, the chemicals of a material body will recombine to form other chemicals. After death, the biochemical makeup of living bodies turns into plants and rich soil. Only God remains outside the cycle of life and death.

Nothing is like God, and God is like nothing. God alone is unique.

THE LIGHT VERSES

The following verses, from surah Nur, are among the most beautiful in the Qur'an.

> God is the Light
> of the heavens and the earth.
> The parable of His Light
> is as if there were a niche
>   and within it a lamp:
> The lamp enclosed in glass,
> the glass [shining] like
> a brilliant star:
> [a lamp] lit from a blessed tree,
> an olive tree, neither of the East
> nor of the West,
> whose oil is well nigh
> luminous,
> though fire had not touched it.
> Light upon Light!
> God guides
> whom He wills
> to His Light,
> And [to this end] God propounds parables to humanity,
> As God [alone] has full knowledge of all things. (24:35)

Traditionally, Muslims studied at night by the light of the oil lamp.

The following commentary on these verses is by Ibn al-Qayyim:

> The "allegory of God's light" signifies "the allegory of God's light in the heart of the Muslim." This is a reference to the light that God sets in the hearts of the servants of God, in the form of knowledge and love of God, belief in God, and remembrance of God. It is also God's light that God sends to human beings; He gives them life by implanting it in their hearts.[5]

The "niche" is the foundation upon which the lamp rests. Before electric lighting, lamps were often set in wall niches designed to reflect light throughout the room. Similarly, the heart is the foundation upon which the soul rests.

The "glass" protects the flame from being put out by a sudden breeze. Glass is made from sand and other opaque materials that are refined and transformed until they become transparent to light. So too, more light flows through us as our personality becomes cleansed and purified. The glass does not possess its own light, but when the light falls upon it, it shines like a brilliant star.

The pure flame is the divine spark within our hearts. Those who have unveiled this flame in themselves can ignite other hearts. The light of truth has existed in all the prophets and in all great spiritual teachers. All God's prophets are essentially the same. Their pure hearts appear to be self-luminous, however, their light is actually a reflection of a single source—divine light.

The olive tree is small and unimpressive compared to many other trees. But the olive fruit makes wholesome food and wonderful oil. The oil is like spiritual truth, which illuminates the mind and heart almost before we have been consciously touched by it.

EXPERIENCE ISLAM

SCRIPTURAL STUDY

Choose one or two verses from the Qur'an to study and contemplate. You can choose from the verses given in this book or get a copy of the Qur'an and choose a verse from it.

Years ago my Sufi master advised me to skim the Qur'an instead of reading it line by line. Whenever a verse caught my attention I was to stop and read it carefully, then contemplate its meaning. My teacher also had me keep a notebook in which I wrote down the verses that most deeply touched me. Once I began this practice, the Qur'an changed from being a collection of obscure historical references and inexplicable passages to a source of great wisdom and inspiration.

TWO EXAMPLES OF CONTEMPLATION

God's Presence One of my favorite verses is "Wherever you turn there is the Face of God" (2:115). I am deeply touched every time I read or recite this phrase. What a wonderful reminder—God is always with us! No matter where we turn, no matter what the circumstances, no matter how dark and depressed things may seem, God's Presence has never left us and will never leave us.

We can find God everywhere and at every moment—in each tree, in every flower, in the sky and the earth, and in the eyes and hearts of everyone we meet. God's Presence is not only everywhere we turn without, but it is also wherever we look within. All we have to do is to part the veils that we have placed between ourselves and God. In a famous *hadith qudsi*, God says, "There may be ten thousand veils between you and Me, but there are no veils between Me and you."

Find a verse that inspires you, and contemplate its various levels of meaning and the ways it inspires or guides you.

Learn from Nature Contemplate the following verses:

> *And God sends down rain from the skies,*
> *giving life to the earth after it had been lifeless;*
> *Behold, in this there is a message for people who listen.*
> *And behold, in cattle too there is indeed a lesson for you:*
> *From what is in their bodies, between excretions and blood,*
> *We give you milk, pure and pleasant to those who drink it.*
> *And from the fruit of date-palms and vines:*
> *From it you get wholesome nourishment or intoxicants.*
> *In this, behold, there is a message indeed for people who use*
> *their reason. (16:65–67)*

God tells us to learn from nature, and many of the greatest spiritual lessons can be learned from God's creation, which is filled with God's *ayahs*, or signs. As the Qur'an teaches, without any effort on our part, cattle provide milk, and trees and vines provide fruit. We can turn that fruit into wholesome food and drink, or we can create from it intoxicants that poison our minds and bodies.

Spend a day in a natural environment, and look around you for similar signs of God's generosity and signs of Divine Truth. At the end of the day, write down everything you have learned.

CHAPTER FOUR

THE HISTORY OF ISLAM

Islamic history is a fourteen hundred year pageant filled with poetry and passion, magnificent contributions to science and medicine, brilliant statesmen, and also oppressive tyrants. Beginning in 610 C.E. with a single, humble merchant in Makkah, within 20 years Islam spread all through Arabia; ten years later, Islam expanded throughout the Middle East. Islam now stretches from Eastern Europe through Asia, all the way to China, Indonesia, and the Philippines.

THE
FOUR CALIPHS

Previous page: Mamaluk minarets tower above the Fatimid courtyard at Al-Azhar Mosque, founded in 972 C.E., in Cairo, Egypt.

After the passing away of the Prophet ﷺ, two important questions arose among his community. Who was to succeed him? How would the rapidly growing Islamic community be governed?

Muhammad ﷺ was loved and revered as God's prophet, and he was considered divinely guided in his political and social decisions. Those who were to follow him would have to rely on their own personal insight and intelligence. Who could fill the Prophet's ﷺ shoes, and how could they maintain the divine truths of Islam in a violent and ever-changing secular world?

Some of the leading Muslims thought each Muslim tribe should select its own leader, a traditional Bedouin custom. The Prophet's ﷺ closest companions, Abu Bakr and Umar, argued that the Islamic community must remain united under a single leader, as it had been under the Prophet ﷺ. Some thought the Prophet ﷺ should be succeeded by Ali, his closest male relative. This was the most common way of selecting a new tribal leader. However, Ali was relatively young and inexperienced in politics, and so the majority voted for Abu Bakr, one of the oldest and most generous Muslims and the Prophet's ﷺ closest friend.

The four men who led the Islamic community after Muhammad ﷺ became known as the four "rightly guided" caliphs. In Arabic, *khalifah* means deputy. The authority of the caliph was rooted in his role as the representative, or regent, of the holy Prophet ﷺ.

IMMEDIATELY AFTER THE PROPHET ﷺ PASSED AWAY, A CROWD GATHERED IN THE MOSQUE. MANY REFUSED TO BELIEVE THE NEWS; OTHERS SAID THAT MUHAMMAD ﷺ WOULD SOON RETURN AND CONTINUE TO GUIDE THE COMMUNITY. ABU BAKR SAID TO THE CROWD: "WHOEVER WORSHIPS MUHAMMAD, LET THEM KNOW THAT MUHAMMAD HAS DIED; BUT WHOEVER WORSHIPS GOD, LET THEM KNOW THAT GOD IS ALIVE AND DOES NOT DIE." [1]

ABU BAKR

Abu Bakr served as caliph from 632 to 634 C.E. This was a particularly critical time for Islam, as many of the tribes that had embraced Islam now sought to break away from the Islamic community and regain their traditional independence.

Abu Bakr managed to put down a series of tribal uprisings and succeeded in unifying Arabia. He virtually doubled the size of the lands controlled by the Muslims. Following the example of the Prophet ﷺ, Abu Bakr was patient and merciful with the rebellious tribes, and pardoned all those who eventually returned to the community of Islam. Already an old man when he became caliph, Abu Bakr unfortunately passed away after serving for only two years.

ABU BAKR'S INAUGURATION SPEECH

People! Even though I am not the best of you, I have been given the responsibility of ruling you . . . O People! I am a follower [of the Prophet], not an innovator. So, if I do well, assist me. And if I deviate, straighten me out. And reckon with yourselves before you are taken to reckoning . . .

Then obey me as long as I obey God! But if I disobey God or his Prophet, you owe me no obedience. I really prefer that another of you should have been given this responsibility. And if you expect me to assume the same role as the Prophet in relation to revelation, I cannot do that. I am only human, so make allowances for me.[2]

UMAR

Umar served as the second caliph for ten years, from 634 to 644 C.E. With the rapid growth of Islam, Islamic society was rapidly changing as well. Umar realized that the old custom of tribal raiding was critical to the survival of many poorer desert tribes. However, now that the Bedouin were unified under Islam, raids among the tribes were treated as attacks against the Islamic community. As an alternative, Umar organized the tribes into a permanent fighting force which boiled out of

Arabia and conquered the entire Middle East.

They invaded Mesopotamia, Syria, and Egypt and, in 637 C.E., defeated the Persian army. By 641 C.E., the Muslims controlled all of Syria, Mesopotamia, Palestine, and Egypt. These military achievements were not "religious wars." The goal was economic, a continuation of the tradition of raiding the Arabian tribes had practiced for centuries. Now, however, the combined tribal raiding parties were far larger and met relatively little resistance from the lands around them.

Umar's era was marked by his straightforward, puritan character. It came to be seen as a golden age by many Muslims, a peaceful age unmarked by the religious and political strife that was to arise later.

UMAR'S ADVICE

Do not be misled by someone's reputation.

Do not judge people only by their performance of prayer and fasting; rather look into their truthfulness and wisdom.

Those who keep their secrets control their affairs.

Fear the person whom you hate.

Prudent are they who can assess their actions.

Do not defer your work for tomorrow.

Those who have no idea of evil can easily fall into its trap.

Judge others' intelligence by the questions they ask.

Less concern for material well-being enables one to lead a free life.

It's easier to indulge in sins than to repent.

Contentment and gratitude are two great virtues.

Be grateful to those who point out your defects.[3]

THE PEOPLE OF THE BOOK

The Muslims did not seek to convert those they conquered. Most of their neighbors were already People of the Book—Jews or Christians. In Muslim eyes, they were already following their own authentic scriptures. For example, when Umar entered Jerusalem, he was invited to pray in one of the great churches. He refused out of respect for Christianity, saying if he prayed in the church, he feared his devoted followers would turn it into a mosque after he had gone.

Jews and Christians were treated as *dhimmis*, or protected subjects. They had complete religious freedom. They were exempt from military service, and instead, they were required to pay a tax in exchange for military protection. Conquered agricultural lands were left in the hands of their original owners, who paid rent to the Muslim state. Conquered cities were basically left alone. Muslim soldiers built their own towns, strategically located Islamic enclaves in the new lands.

UTHMAN

After Umar, Uthman became the third caliph (644–656 C.E.). He had a gentle character and was loved by the people. Uthman established an official version of the Qur'an, which had previously existed in several variants. Uthman was one of the earliest Muslims. One night he heard a voice saying, "Sleepers awake! For Ahmad [Muhammad] has come forth in Makkah." He consulted Abu Bakr who brought him to the Prophet ﷺ. Uthman established an official version of the Qur'an, which had previously existed in several versions.

Muslim armies continued to expand into new lands, including much of North Africa, Afghanistan, and western India. As a result of all these conquests, Muslim society was changing. The younger men no longer lived like their desert nomad ancestors. They

Right: A Suni Muslim man, Bukhara, Uzbekistan.

UMAR REMEMBERS DEATH

Umar hired a man to remind him of death. Every day the man would come to him and say, "O caliph, remember death. It is coming to you and to all of us." One day, Umar called the man in and paid him his usual stipend along with a bonus. Umar said, "Thank you for your service, but I will not be needing you any more." Startled, the man asked if he had offended the caliph or done something wrong. "No," replied Umar, "I do not need your services any more. This morning I found a white hair in my beard."

were now members of a disciplined, full-time army spread over vast distances.

Uthman refused requests by the military commanders and powerful Muslim families to take over conquered territory as their own private estates. He also alienated many of the prominent families of Madinah by appointing members of his own Umayyad clan to the most powerful and prestigious positions in the new Muslim empire. Uthman was not as strict as Umar and did not strongly oppose the corruption of some of the Muslim governors. Some of the corrupt governors were from his own clan, and others had become so powerful they simply ignored Uthman's authority as caliph.

When a group of petitioners from various provinces traveled to Madinah to complain of their corrupt governors, Uthman put them off. Their discontent turned to rebellion, fanned by a false rumor that Uthman was plotting to have them all killed once they returned home. The group broke into Uthman's house and assassinated him. Then the assassins proclaimed Ali as the new caliph.

ALI

Many Muslims were shocked at the killing of Uthman, who was one of the earliest Muslims and, like Ali , had been a son-in-law of the Prophet ﷺ. After Ali became caliph, he was urged to punish Uthman's killers. However, many of Ali's strongest supporters argued that Uthman had deserved death because he had not ruled justly, chosing Muslim leaders from his own clan.

Ali did not rush to punish the killers, nor did he condemn Uthman. He delayed his decision until he could investigate more fully and tempers had cooled down somewhat. Some thought that this meant he refused to bring the killers to justice. Those who insisted on immediate punishment became impatient and formed an army of rebels, led by the Prophet's ﷺ widow Aishah. Ali's supporters easily defeated the rebels, but the unity of the Islamic community was now broken.

Ali decided to replace every governor appointed by Uthman. The new leader of the Umayyad clan, Muawiyah, was also the governor of Syria. Muawiyah refused to step down as governor or to accept Ali as the new caliph. Muawiyah took his army into Arabia, ostensibly to punish the murderers of Uthman. Ali and his army met them, and after three days of battle, Ali's army was clearly

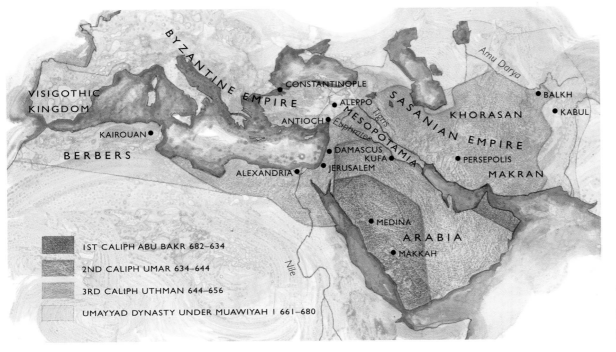

1ST CALIPH ABU BAKR 682–634

2ND CALIPH UMAR 634–644

3RD CALIPH UTHMAN 644–656

UMAYYAD DYNASTY UNDER MUAWIYAH I 661–680

The expansion of the Muslim empire in 656 C.E..

winning. Muawiyah had his soldiers hang pages from the Qur'an on the ends of their spears to hold off Ali's troops. His scheme worked. Ali held off his attack, not wanting to dishonor the Qur'an, and agreed to negotiate.

A group of soldiers defected from Ali's camp because they felt that Ali should have continued the battle and destroyed the rebels. They were also upset that Ali had failed to right the wrongs committed by Uthman and had given in to Muawiyah and the other supporters of injustice. These rebels, known as Kharijites, or seceders, believed that the caliph, as the religious leader of Islam, had to be the most pious and righteous Muslim. Despite their army being defeated by Ali's forces, their movement spread throughout the Muslim community. In 661 C.E., Ali was murdered by one of the Kharijites.

Muawiyah appointed himself as caliph and tried to reunite the Muslim community from his new capital in Damascus. The shift of power to Damascus symbolized the end of an era. The united Muslim community, under the guidance of a prophet, was now a thing of the past as was the era of the four devout, rightly guided caliphs, who had been among the closest companions of the Prophet ﷺ.

"OH PEOPLE, YOUR GOD IS ONE AND YOU HAVE A SINGLE FATHER, ADAM. WHOEVER IS MORE PIOUS IS MORE ELEVATED, AND NO ONE IS SUPERIOR BECAUSE HE IS AN ARAB OR NON-ARAB, BUT ONLY THROUGH HIS PIETY." MUHAMMAD ﷺ 4

Muawiyah ruled as caliph from 661 to 680 C.E.. He continued to maintain the separation of the Arab Muslims from the local populations and continued to discourage conversion to Islam. Personally a devout Muslim, Muawiyah did his very best to maintain the unity of the Muslim community.

ALI'S CHARACTER

One day, the Prophet ﷺ posed a question to Abu Bakr and Ali. He asked, "What would you do if someone deliberately did something to hurt you, and then they apologized?" Both immediately said they would forgive the person.

"What would you do if the person hurt you the same way a second time, and then apologized again?" Both men agreed they would forgive the person again.

"What would you do if the person hurt you the same way a third time, and apologized yet again?" Both men said they would forgive the person once again.

"What would you do if the person hurt you the same way a fourth time, and then apologized again?" Abu Bakr remained silent, but Ali said he would still forgive the person.

The Prophet ﷺ kept asking, and each time Ali said he would continue to forgive the person who had hurt him. Finally, the Prophet ﷺ asked, "How long would you go on forgiving this person?" Ali replied, "Until either the person dies or I die."

On hearing this last reply from Ali, the Prophet ﷺ smiled.

THE UMAYYAD
DYNASTY

Muawiyah appointed his son Yazid as his successor, despite opposition from many Muslims who felt that their leaders should be elected according to Arab traditions. In the Iraqi city of Kufah, Muslims still loyal to Ali claimed Ali's son Hussain should be caliph and invited him to lead them. Hussain left Madinah with a small band of followers and their families. In 681 C.E., on the plain of Karbala outside Kufah, they were surrounded by Yazid's Umayyad troops and all of them were massacred. Today, Muslims still mourn the martyrdom of the Prophet's beloved grandson, Hussain.

In western Arabia, rebels against the Umayyads sought a return to the purity of the early days of Islam. In central Arabia, Kharijite forces set up an independent state, and there were Kharijite uprisings in Iraq and Iran as well. In 691 C.E., after eight years of struggle, the uprisings were put down and unity was restored by the Syrian forces of Abd al-Malik, a cousin of Muawiyah. Abd al-Malik ruled as Umayyad caliph until his death in 705 C.E. After the rebels were quelled, his reign was peaceful and prosperous. Arabic replaced Persian as the official state language. The old segregation between Muslim troops and the local populations began to break down. In 691, the Dome of the Rock in Jerusalem, the first great Islamic monument, was completed. This was the beginning of a new tradition of distinctively Islamic architecture.

Political and religious discussions centered on how to practice Islam in this new era. Was it Islamic for the Umayyad court to live in luxury while so many were poor? What did it really mean to be a Muslim? Should the Islamic community welcome non-Arab converts and become an Islamic rather than an Arab community? These intense debates were to shape the practice of Islam from the eighth century until today.

A revival of Islamic spirituality was begun by Hasan al-Basri (died 728 C.E.). Hasan grew up in Madinah, close to the Prophet's ﷺ family. He advocated a simple, ascetic lifestyle, similar to that of the Prophet ﷺ. Hasan taught his followers to meditate on the inner meaning of the Qur'an and to seek to surrender fully to God's Will. This is generally considered to be the beginning of the Islamic spiritual movement called *tasawwuf*, known in the West as Sufism. Although Hasan and his followers deplored the luxury and license of the Umayyad court, they accepted the Umayyad caliphate in order to preserve the unity of the Muslim community. In this, they differed from the Kharijites, who still remained totally opposed to Umayyad rule.

The al-Aqsa Mosque and the Dome of the Rock, the third holiest site in Islam.

In 707 C.E., 75 years after the death of Muhammad ﷺ, the Umayyad caliphate funded the first hospital in Damascus. The doctors were paid by government funds, and the hospital provided a full range of free medical services. It became a model for hospitals and medical centers throughout the Islamic world.

Statue of Averroës, Córdoba, Spain.

All doctors trained in these hospitals and they were all required to pass a series of medical examinations. By the eleventh century, free medical care was available in rural areas and to the poor in the inner cities.

MUSLIM SPAIN

The Umayyad conquest of North Africa expanded to the conquest of most of Spain and the establishment of a Muslim Spanish kingdom by 750 C.E. Spain became a center of interchange between Muslim, Jewish, and Christian scholars. Many of the great works of Greek philosophy and medicine entered Europe through this interchange. The cities of Córdoba and Granada became great centers of art and learning.

By the tenth century, Córdoba, the capital city of Muslim Spain, was one of the greatest cities in the world. At this time, cities like London and Paris had dirt streets and no sanitation. Córdoba had clean, paved, well-lit streets and running water. There were 70 libraries, and the largest, the sultan's library, contained 400,000 volumes. The Great Mosque of Córdoba was regarded as an architectural masterpiece.

The writings of the great Spanish Muslim Cordoban philosopher Ibn Rushd, known in the West as Averroës, influenced Western philosophers for over four centuries.

After centuries of religious coexistence, the Inquisition and the rise of Christian militancy led to the reconquest of Spain, which was completed in 1492 C.E.. Muslims and Jews were forced to accept Christianity or to go into exile. Many Jews emigrated to Ottoman Turkey, where the sultans welcomed them and allowed them complete freedom of trade and of religion. Sultan Beyezid II commented, "Spain's loss is my gain."

AVERROËS, THE GREAT PHILOSOPHER

Ibn Rushd, or Averroës, is known in the West primarily for his commentaries on Aristotle. He influenced most thinkers in the Middle Ages, including Maimonides and Thomas Aquinas.

Ibn Rushd was born in Córdoba, Spain, in 1126 C.E. and spent most of his life as a judge and as a physician. Ibn Rushd wrote on philosophy, logic, medicine, music, and law. He wrote 78 books, including 20 books on medicine. He wrote an astronomical treatise on spherical motion, and he is also credited with the discovery of sunspots. His book on law has been considered by some as the best book on the Maliki School of jurisprudence. He became best known for his brilliant commentaries on Aristotle. Many of his books are still preserved today.

Ibn Rushd believed that Islam aims at true knowledge, which consists of both knowledge of God and knowledge of God's Creation. He compared spiritual laws to medicine; medicine seeks to bring about physical health, and religion aims to bring moral and spiritual health. Ibn Rushd's writings were translated into many languages, including Latin, English, German, and Hebrew. He had a major influence on Western thought from the twelfth to the sixteenth century.

THE ABBASID DYNASTY

In 750 C.E., the Abbasid clan overthrew the Umayyids and took over the caliphate. Baghdad became the new capital of the Islamic empire. As time went by, the caliphs became more and more like monarchs. The most famous Abbasid caliph was Harun ar-Rashid (786–809 C.E.). He was an absolute ruler, isolated from his subjects and surrounded by an aristocratic court. Harun was a great patron of artists and scholars, and, under his rule, philosophy, literature, poetry, medicine, mathematics, and astronomy flourished. He sponsored translations into Arabic of the great Greek works of classical philosophy and medicine.

Harun found it was impossible to rule the vast territory of the Islamic empire. He tried to solve this problem by dividing the empire between his two sons. His solution backfired, resulting in a civil war after his death. The victorious son became the new caliph. Besides the civil war, he had to contend with a Shiah rebellion and a Kharijite uprising as well.

The Abbasid caliphs tried, without success, to reach out to the Shiahs and to the other religious factions that developed. Rebellions by Shiah and other groups continued. The empire suffered politically and economically.

SHIAH ISLAM

Two distinct traditions began to take form within Islam. One, the Shiah tradition, dates back to the time of the four caliphs. The original supporters of Ali were known as Partisans of Ali, or *Shiat Ali*. They were the most deeply aggrieved by the martyrdom

Ribat of Monastir, Tunisia. Built during the Abbasid Dynasty.

of Ali's son Hussain, and believed that the caliphate should have been reserved for the Prophet's ﷺ descendants. The more radical Shiahs blamed all the problems of Islam on the first three caliphs. They felt Ali should have succeeded the Prophet ﷺ. Some even held that Ali was an incarnation of God.

The Shiahs count Ali as the First Imam, or religious leader, and his sons Hasan and Hussain as the Second and Third Imams. They believe a hidden body of knowledge was passed through the line of Ali's descendants, and only one those who received this knowledge could become the next Imam. Jafar al-Sadiq, the Sixth Imam, declared that as Imam he was the true religious leader of Islam, but he would not claim to be caliph, or secular leader, as well. Jafar's school of jurisprudence became the legal school followed by all the Shiahs.

"SEEKING KNOWLEDGE IS BETTER THAN WORSHIP." MUHAMMAD ﷺ 6

The Shiahs split into two major branches. The Ismailis accept only the first eight Imams. The Twelve Shiahs accept the first twelve Imams. When the Eleventh Imam died in 873 C.E., the identity of the Twelfth Imam remained a mystery. In 935 C.E., Shiah clerics declared that the Twelfth Imam had been concealed from this world by God, and would remain hidden until the time came for him to return and bring about a new era of justice and piety. From this time on, the Shiah *ulama*, the body of learned religious teachers, were considered representatives of the Hidden Imam.

SUNNI ISLAM

The majority of Muslims, the Sunnis, insisted that the Shariah, Islamic law, be based primarily on the Qur'an and the example (*sunnah*) of the Prophet ﷺ. The more conservative insisted on meticulously following the Prophet's ﷺ example in all things. They would trim their beards and moustaches as he did, wash, eat, and sleep as he did. This group was known as the People of the Hadith; they insisted that Islamic law must be strictly based on *hadith*, the record of the teachings and actions of the Prophet ﷺ. The People of the Hadith were deeply conservative, idealizing the times of the Prophet ﷺ and the early caliphs.

A major figure at this time was Abu Hanifah, a great religious scholar who developed the new discipline of Islamic law. He built a legal system on the teachings of the Qur'an plus the example (*sunnah*) and the teachings (*hadith*) of the Prophet ﷺ.

Abu Hanifah established the first of four great Sunni schools of jurisprudence. These schools developed to handle the new problems and questions of a far larger and more complex Islamic society. Abu Hanifah insisted that Islamic law must be built with the help of *ijtihad*, independent reasoning. For him and his followers, new laws could be developed to fit new times, built on Islamic principles, even if such laws were not directly based on a *hadith* or Qur'anic example.

The second major school of jurisprudence, the Maliki school, was based on the laws, customs, and religious practices of Madinah. The Malikis believe that Madinah had preserved the original culture and practices of the Prophet's ﷺ community. The third school, the Shafii school, argued that instead of relying on a single city, laws should be based primarily on the *hadith*. The Shafiis carefully studied the collections of *hadith* and weeded out all *hadith* for which the chain of witnesses was broken or unreliable. They allowed a small degree of *ijtihad*, limited to making analogies from *hadith* to contemporary issues. The fourth major school, the Hanbali school, developed last, and was closest to the People of the Hadith.

The Abbasids supported the development of religious law for the whole empire. One basic element in the Shariah is egalitarianism. All Muslims are considered equal before God. No religious authority can come between the individual and their relation to God, and each Muslim individually responsible for following God's commands.

"THE LEARNED ARE LIKE THE STARS IN THE SKY THAT SHINE AND GUIDE TRAVELERS ON SEA AND ON EARTH. WHEN THE STARS DISAPPEAR, EVEN THOSE WHO HAVE FOUND THEIR WAY MAY LOSE THEIR DIRECTION."

MUHAMMAD ﷺ 7

THE DIVIDED EMPIRE

By the tenth century, the empire was irrevocably split. The caliph was still the symbolic head of the community of Islam, but no longer the political ruler of the entire community. In Egypt, the Ismaili Shiah Fatimids set up their own caliphate in Cairo. The Fatimids came to rule North Africa, Syria, Palestine, and eastern Arabia. Their army was composed primarily of Mamluks, Turkish slaves who converted to Islam. In time, Mamluk generals seized power in Iraq, Iran, and Central Asia.

The Abbasid caliph continued to rule in Baghdad and was still acknowledged as religious leader. In 1055, when the Seljuk Turks took power in Baghdad, they ruled as the caliph's "lieutenants." Nomadic Turkish cavalry formed the basis of Seljuk military power. Turkish horse-archers were highly skilled marksmen. Their recurved bows, made from layers of horn, sinew, and wood, had an even greater range than the famed English longbow.

Many of the independent Muslim states began to flourish. The Fatimid capital of Cairo became a great center of art and scholarship, and the college of al-Azhar was founded there, eventually to become the finest Islamic school in the world.

The Seljuks continued to expand. By 1071, the Seljuk empire reached to Yemen in the south, Syria in the west, and Afghanistan in the east. Local military governors ruled each district of the empire, along with the Muslim clergy, the *ulama*. The Seljuks were nomads and had little interest in the conquered lands or their people; the *ulama* held the provinces together.

Religious schools, *madrasas*, were established throughout the Seljuk empire, and provided formal training for the *ulama*. Local power became firmly vested in the *ulama*, backed by the authority of the Qur'an, and Sunni Islam became stronger throughout the empire.

The Prophet ﷺ said:

"A scholar whose knowledge benefits others is worthier than thousands of worshipers." Muhammad ﷺ [9]

"THE CURE FOR IGNORANCE IS TO ASK AND LEARN." MUHAMMAD ﷺ [8]

ISLAMIC LAW: THE SHARIAH

The Shariah is based primarily on two basic sources—the Qur'an and the sunnah of the Prophet ﷺ. Because the Prophet's ﷺ whole life was divinely guided, following his example—being kind and charitable to others, acting with courtesy and consideration, valuing cleanliness, etc.—guarantees that one is behaving as God wishes. The Qur'an, as God's Word, is considered infinite in its depth of meaning, as God is infinite. Every line of the Qur'an contains many levels of meaning, and the revelation of the Qur'an is considered to speak directly to Muslims in every age.

The Sunnis considered the unity of the community of Islam a sacred value. Muslims were encouraged to support the caliphs as representatives of that unity, even if their government was imperfect.

THE ASSASSINS

In the 1090s, a radical group of Ismaili Shiahs dedicated themselves to the destruction of the Seljuks and Sunni Islam. They made their headquarters in a mountain fortress in Alamut in Syria. The Ismailis raided the Seljuks and also murdered many of the military governors, especially those who were corrupt and oppressed

> ## THE MONGOLS
>
> *By the end of the twelfth century, Ghengis Khan managed to unite the Mongol tribes into the most powerful military force the world had ever known.*
>
> *The Mongol hordes were the scourge of the Muslim world. They destroyed thousands of priceless manuscripts, monuments, and works of art and massacred over sixteen million people in Persia and Iraq alone. By 1258 C.E., the Abbasid caliphate and the city of Baghdad were wiped out by the Mongols.*
>
> *From the early thirteenth century until the mid- to late fourteenth century, the Mongols established four great states in the Middle East and Russia. In the Far East, Kublai Khan ruled virtually all of China. The Mongols were tolerant of all religions, and, by the beginning of the fourteenth century, all four western Mongol states converted to Islam. Traditional Mongol values persisted however, focusing on military power and conquest.*
>
> *As the Mongols gradually moved from nomadic to city life, they rebuilt, more splendidly than before, many of the cities they had destroyed. The new Mongol courts became centers of art, science, mathematics, and history.*

the population. Seljuk officials were generally killed by a single Ismaili wielding a dagger, knowing he was going to be killed in turn by the official's bodyguard. These rebels became known as *hashishin*, because they were believed to use hashish to give themselves the courage to embrace certain death. This is the root of the Western term assassin.

The assassins spread an underground network throughout the Seljuk empire. They built their own state surrounding Alamut, which lasted well over a hundred years until the Mongol invasions that began in 1220 C.E.. Their actions failed to overthrow the Seljuks because most Muslims were completely opposed to their terror tactics. Many innocent Ismailis and other Shiahs were killed, and the Shiah tradition in general was discredited.

THE CRUSADES

In 1099 C.E., Christian European armies invaded Jerusalem, the third holiest city in Islam after Makkah and Madinah. It had been under Muslim rule for over four hundred years, during which time large Jewish and Christian communities lived and worshipped peacefully. The Crusaders slaughtered the entire population—Muslims, Jews, and Christians alike. They established strongholds in Palestine, Syria, Lebanon, and Anatolia.

In 1187 C.E., the great Muslim general Saladin retook Jerusalem. He defeated the Crusader armies, although several small Crusader states remained.

THE MONGOL INVASION

When Genghis Khan united the Mongol tribes, he became the leader of a vast, unstoppable force that obliterated any who resisted. In 1258 C.E., the Abbasid caliphate and the city of Baghdad were completely destroyed by the Mongols. It took the Mongols forty days to execute the whole population of Baghdad.

DECLINE OF THE
MONGOL STATES

The Mongol states began to decline by the late fourteenth century. At this time, a Turkish general, Timur, came to power. He was called Timur the lame because of his limp and was known in the West as Tamerlane. He began to conquer the western Mongol states and then invaded India and sacked Delhi. In 1404 C.E., Timur invaded China where he was killed.

At the same time, the Ottoman Turks were expanding in Anatolia. By the end of the fourteenth century, they occupied most of the territory of the old Byzantine empire and advanced into the Balkans, conquering the kingdoms of Bulgaria and Serbia. They were defeated by Timur in 1402 C.E., but regained power after his death. In 1453 C.E., the Ottoman sultan Mehmed II conquered Constantinople itself.

By the end of the fifteenth century, Islam had spread to eastern Europe, into the steppes of Central Asia, and throughout large portions of Africa. Islam was the major religion of the Middle East, northern India, and Malaya. Islam was originally introduced to China in 681 C.E., and some ancient Chinese mosques that are over a thousand years old remain. The population of Muslims in China eventually grew to many millions.

Muslim traders brought Islam to Indonesia as early as 665 C.E. and Islam was spread primarily by wandering Sufi teachers. Today, Indonesia has the largest Muslim population in the world.

The late fifteenth century was the time of the rise of three great Islamic empires: the Safavid empire of Persia, the Mughal empire in India, and the Ottoman empire, which eventually spread from eastern Europe through Anatolia and Syria, and included North Africa and Arabia as well.

Wall tiles on the mihrab (niche indicating direction of Makkah) of the mosque of Cheykhoun (fourteenth century).

The great Mongol states spread from Russia through China, 1255–1265 C.E..

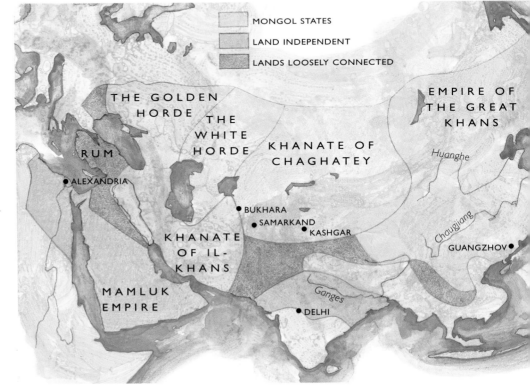

MONGOL STATES
LAND INDEPENDENT
LANDS LOOSELY CONNECTED

THE GOLDEN HORDE

THE WHITE HORDE

EMPIRE OF THE GREAT KHANS

RUM

●ALEXANDRIA

KHANATE OF CHAGHATEY

Huanghe

●BUKHARA
●SAMARKAND
●KASHGAR

KHANATE OF IL-KHANS

Chaugjiang

GUANGZHOV●

MAMLUK EMPIRE

Ganges

●DELHI

THE SAFAVID
EMPIRE OF IRAN

This great empire was founded by a Sufi mystical order. The Safavid Sufi Order followed the Shiah tradition and was located in Azerbaijan. In 1500 C.E., sixteen-year-old Ismail became head of the order at the death of his father, who had been killed by the Seljuks. He founded the Safavid empire. Ismail began a military campaign to avenge his father. In 1501 C.E., he conquered the city of Tabriz, and, in the next ten years, Ismail went on to conquer the rest of Iran.

Shah Ismail claimed to be a descendant of the Shiah Imams, and he began to drive out the Sunni ulama. He established Shiah Islam as the religion of Iran, which had been primarily Sunni.

At the turn of the seventeenth century, Shah Abbas I extended the Iranian empire and strengthened Iranian Shiah Islam by importing Arab Shiah ulama and building a network of Shiah madrasas. His court was a center of art and culture. The great painters of Persian miniatures flourished at this time. The capital city of Isfahan was filled with stunning mosques and palaces, great madrasas, and lovely parks and gardens.

The Iranian Shiah tradition replaced Sufi chanting and devotional ceremonies with annual rituals mourning the martyrdom of the Prophet's grandson Hussain. The people treated this tragedy as if it had just happened. There were highly emotional processions in which many participants whipped themselves into a frenzy of grief as onlookers beat their breasts and cried out and wept uncontrollably.

By the late seventeenth century the Iranian empire had declined and was severely weakened economically. In 1722 C.E., Afghan tribes took Isfahan. They were defeated by an Iranian general, Nadir Khan, who then made himself shah—the monarch. A brilliant general but a ruthless ruler, Nadir Khan was assassinated in 1748 C.E..

Following Nadir Khan's death, in the absence of a central government, the Shiah ulama gained even greater power. They promoted the doctrine that ordinary Muslims were incapable of understanding Islam by themselves. The people needed the guidance of the ulama, who alone had the inner understanding of the Qur'an derived from the Hidden Imam. This gave the Iranian ulama a degree of religious authority and control never known before in Islam.

"GOODNESS WILL NEITHER GROW OLD NOR FADE AWAY; WICKEDNESS WILL NOT BE FORGOTTEN, AND THE GOD OF A JUST PERSON WILL NEVER DIE. DO WHATEVER YOU WISH, BUT REMEMBER THAT YOU WILL RECEIVE WHATEVER YOU CULTIVATE."

MUHAMMAD ﷺ 10

THE MUGHAL EMPIRE

The founder of the Mughal empire, Babur (1483–1530 C.E.), was a direct descendent of Timur on his father's side and of Genghis Khan on his mother's side. Babur's father died when he was only 12, and he became ruler of his father's small kingdom, which lay in a valley east of Samarkand. He dreamed of re-establishing his ancestor Timur's empire.

After several unsuccessful campaigns to conquer the great walled city of Samarkand, Babur and three hundred poorly equipped followers set off for Kabul. The local ruler fled and, in 1504 C.E., Babur took over Kabul and the surrounding area.

Babur sought to expand his kingdom and began a series of expeditions to invade India. In 1526 C.E., he challenged the Sultan of Delhi, the most powerful ruler in India. Babur's force of under 10,000 warriors faced an army of 100,000 plus 100 battle elephants. Babur's overwhelming victory paved the way for his conquest of central India.

In a letter to his eldest son, Babur gave the following advice on rulership:

> "Do not fail to make the most of an opportunity that presents itself. Indolence and luxury do not suit kingship. Conquest tolerates not inaction; the world is his who hastens most. When one is master one may rest from everything—except being king." [11]

Babur is perhaps best known as a writer and a poet. His memoirs were translated into English in the early nineteenth century. Noted writer Francis Robinson wrote, "What a happiness to have known

The extraordinary balance and beauty of the Taj Mahal make it one of the world's most magnificent buildings.

Babur! He had all that one seeks in a friend. His energy and ambition were touched with sensitiveness; he could act, observe, and remember." [12]

In 1560 C.E., Babur's grandson Akbar became the Mughal emperor. He continued to govern in the old Mongol ("Mughal") tradition, in which the central government was run as an army under his direct command. An efficient bureaucracy and an army well equipped with firearms enabled Akbar to expand his empire throughout most of India.

Akbar was a highly tolerant ruler. He did not attempt to convert his subjects to Islam. In fact, he became a vegetarian and gave up hunting (which he loved) in order to be more like his Hindu subjects. Akbar abolished the tax on non-Muslims and welcomed Hindus into his armies and administration. He built Hindu temples as well as mosques, and also built a non-sectarian house of worship for interaction and discussion among representatives of all religions.

SHAH JAHAN AND SHAH AURANGZEB

Akbar's grandson Shah Jahan (1592–1666 C.E.) expanded Mughal rule throughout most of the Indian subcontinent. He is best known for constructing the Taj Mahal, a blend of the best of Muslim and Hindu architecture, and one of the most beautiful buildings in the world. Shah Jahan brought craftsmen and builders from all over India and from Persia, Turkey, and even Venice to build the Taj Mahal. The central dome is over 23 stories high, and the while marble, inlaid with Qur'anic calligraphy, reflects the shifting light of the day. The harmony of the building itself, set off by exquisite gardens and reflecting pools, has never been equaled.

Jahan's son, Shah Aurangzeb, ruled from 1658 to 1707 C.E.. He spent 26 years subduing the independent Hindu and Muslim states in the south. Aurangzeb rejected the tolerance and universalism inaugurated by Akbar. He destroyed many Hindu temples, taxed non-Muslims heavily, and also persecuted the Shiah Muslim communities in India.

As a result, major revolts broke out, and the Mughal empire never recovered. After Aurangzeb, central authority was so weakened that local officials began to rule independently, and the rebels continued to defy Mughal rule. In 1730 C.E., the Persian ruler, Nadir Shah, invaded northern India, sacked Delhi, and plundered its priceless Mughal treasures. The British, who entered India as traders, began to take political power, eventually to dominate the subcontinent. One by one they brought the princely states of India under their control. By the early nineteenth century, the weakened Mughal emperors were forced to seek British protection.

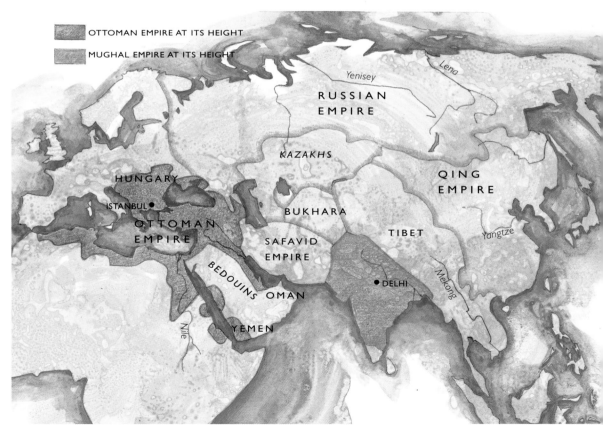

OTTOMAN EMPIRE AT ITS HEIGHT

MUGHAL EMPIRE AT ITS HEIGHT

The Mughal and Ottoman empires at their height.

THE
OTTOMAN EMPIRE

Uthman I (1280–1324 C.E.) founded the Ottoman dynasty. He and his nomad followers settled in central Anatolia. They conquered lands held by Byzantine nobles and moved into Seljuk territories as the Seljuk empire collapsed. The Ottomans expanded north to the Black Sea and west to the Sea of Marmara. In 1326 C.E. they conquered the Byzantine city of Bursa and made it their capital. With the conquest of Bursa, the Ottomans shifted from a nomadic culture to an organized state with a capital, administration, and a settled population.

The Ottomans continued to expand throughout most of Anatolia and then into the Balkans—Thrace, Macedonia, Bulgaria, and Serbia—bypassing Christian Constantinople.

The Ottoman government and military were organized according to Central Asian traditions similar to those of the Mongols. They followed the Mongol concept that the power and core of the state was the army, which was personally commanded by the ruler. Another major influence was Sunni Islam and the legacy of the early Islamic empires and the Seljuks. A third influence came from the Byzantine tradition and the existing Byzantine society, which the Ottomans assimilated.

The early Ottoman sultans had to contend with a series of threats on the borders of their far-flung empire. This included revolts by Balkan princes in the west and declarations of independence by Anatolian governors in the east.

The elite Ottoman troops were the Janissaries. They were Christian levies who were converted to

SULEIMAN THE MAGNIFICENT

Sultan Suleiman's court architect Sinan designed some of the world's greatest mosques and other buildings and set the tone for Ottoman architecture. His masterpiece, the Suleimaniye Mosque in Istanbul, commands the old city and includes Qur'anic schools, four madrasas, a medical college, a hospital, and a library. The Ottoman court sponsored art, medicine, architecture, science, and history, and encouraged a lively interchange with Western ideas.

The empire included many different civilizations, traditions, and peoples—Jews, Arabs, Berbers, Turks, Turcomans, Bosnians, Serbs, and dozens more. Each community was free to follow its own beliefs and customs. Sultan Suleiman was known to his own people as the "Law Giver." He built a system of justice and emphasized protection of the lives, property, and rights of all people, regardless of religion or ethnic group.

The great Suleimaniye Mosque dominates the skyline of Istanbul.

Islam and trained as soldiers and administrators. They had no other ties or allegiances other than their loyalty to the sultan and formed the backbone of the sultan's power. The Ottomans saw themselves as a frontier state, surrounded by potentially hostile Christians in the west and Shiah Safavids in the east.

In 1453 C.E., Sultan Mehmed II conquered Constantinople, which became the new capital of the Ottoman empire. This gave Mehmed II and his successors rulership over the old Byzantine empire, bringing them even greater status.

Sultan Selim I ruled from 1512 to 1520 C.E.. He was one of the greatest conquerors in Islamic history. In his eight-year rule, he built an Ottoman navy, stopped the expanding Safavids by taking over most of eastern Anatolia, and also conquered Moldavia, Syria, Egypt, Algeria, and Arabia.

He was followed by the greatest of the Ottoman sultans, Sultan Suleiman, known in the West as Suleiman the Magnificent. Suleiman added to the empire the rest of north Africa, Yemen, Iraq, Hungary, and Transylvania. Suleiman was a great administrator as well as a great general. He centralized and unified the administration of one of the world's greatest empires.

The Ottoman empire was governed by *pashas* (generals) who each ruled a province. The government was the most sophisticated and efficient of its time. Shariah was the official law of the empire. Well-trained judges were appointed by the sultan to administer justice throughout the empire. The brightest *madrasa* students were admitted to the *ulama* and were backed by Shariah law and the government. They became strong government supporters throughout the empire.

Trade was the life blood of the empire. Silk Road caravans had brought a constant flow of spices, exotic goods, and gold from China to Istanbul, but the caravan trade began to decline in the eighteenth century as European traders discovered sea routes to the East and were able to transport goods by boat more cheaply, safely, and rapidly than by caravan. Ottoman economy began to weaken, military discipline declined, and government corruption grew.

In addition, the *ulama* became more conservative, opposing most of the new ideas.

A CHRONOLOGY OF ISLAMIC HISTORY

632–634 C.E. Caliphate of Abu Bakr

634–644 C.E. Caliphate of Umar

638 C.E. Muslims conquer Jerusalem.

641 C.E. Muslim armies conquer Mesopotamia, Syria, Palestine, and Egypt.

644–656 C.E. Caliphate of Uthman

656–661 C.E. Caliphate of Ali

661–750 C.E. The Umayyad dynasty

681 C.E. Martyrdom of Hussain at Karbala

750–1055 C.E. The Abbasid dynasty

1055–1118 The Seljuk empire

1220–1231 First Mongol raids

1227–1390 Mongol states develop; Mongols convert to Islam.

1369–1405 Timur conquers most of the Middle East and invades India.

1403–1421 Mehmed I revives Ottoman power in Anatolia.

1463 Mehmed II takes Constantinople; renamed Istanbul it becomes capital of the Ottoman empire.

1501 Ismail establishes the Safavid empire in Iran and makes Shiah Islam the state religion.

1526 Babur founds the Mughal empire in India.

1858 The British depose the last Mughal emperor.

1923 Kemal Atatürk wins the Turkish War of Independence and ends the Ottoman sultanate.

1925 Reza Khan overthrows the old dynasty and proclaims himself Shah of Iran.

EXPERIENCE ISLAM

REMEMBER DEATH

As mentioned earlier in this chapter, Caliph Umar paid someone to remind him of death, until he found a white hair in his beard. In Islam as in all the great religions, remembering death allows us to keep a balanced perspective on life. To the extent we deny the reality and inevitability of death, we are likely to overvalue the transient things of this world.

A religious man once went to a saint and asked why he got no pleasure from his prayers. The saint replied it was because the man's heart was closed. The man asked why his heart had become closed, and the saint replied it was because he loved the world too much. The man then asked why he had come to love the world so much, and the saint said it was because he did not remember death.

The saint advised the man to visit hospitals and graveyards and to attend funerals in order to learn to remember death. Some weeks later, the man returned and said that he did what the saint suggested, but it made no difference. He still got no pleasure from his prayers.

The saint told the man that he did not carry out his instructions properly. "Don't go to graveyards and hospitals as an uninvolved observer. When you are in the hospital, look at those who are gravely ill and remind yourself that you will be on a bed like that soon enough, a bed from which you will never get up. When you are in a graveyard, remind yourself that soon enough your body will lie under a headstone just like all those around you. And when you attend a funeral, look at the casket and remind yourself that you will lie in a casket just like that and that there will be a funeral service for you, soon enough."

Some time later the man returned and thanked the saint. His prayers had changed as he began to remember death.

The prescription of the saint is still good today. There are many ways to remember death, as Caliph Umar discovered. Medieval philosophers often kept a skull on their desks as a *memento mori*, a reminder of death. A computer screen saver can serve as a modern version. A picture of a deceased relative, of a casket or gravestone can serve as a reminder that we are only here for a limited time.

For a week, make sure that you are reminded of death at least once a day. Notice how this reminder affects your daily attitudes and activities, and also how you feel at the end of this week.

It is an Islamic tradition to visit the graves of parents and close relatives on religious holidays.

CHAPTER FIVE

SUFISM: THE PATH OF ISLAMIC MYSTICISM

Sufism is the mystical core of Islam.[1] It first appeared as a separate discipline within Islam in the eighth century, with the teachings of Hasan al-Basri. Sufis also describe Sufism as the universal mystical dimension of all religions. For the Sufis, religion is a tree, the roots of which are outward religious practices. The branches of the tree are mysticism, and the fruit is Truth. All mysticism has the same goal: the direct experience of God.

"THE THING WE TELL OF CAN NEVER BE FOUND BY SEEKING, YET ONLY SEEKERS FIND IT."

BAYAZID BISTAMI

Previous page:
Whirling dervishes,
Konya, Turkey.

Mysticism comes from the Greek root *myein*, "to close the eyes," which is also the root of "mystery." Mystics of all religions seek to uncover the same divine mystery, a mystery that is hidden both within and without. My Sufi master used to say, "Mysticism is like a river that flows through many countries. Sometimes it goes underground and then emerges elsewhere, unexpectedly. Different nations give it different names, but it is the same river, wherever it flows."

The mystics are those who seek to know God. They dedicate their lives to traveling the Path of Truth. God is Truth (*ya Haqq*, one of the 99 Names, or Attributes, of God in Arabic). God is the goal and also the Guide (*ya Hadi*). God says in the Qur'an, "All things return to Me," but the Sufis are impatient. They seek union with God now, in this life.

The practice of Sufism varies widely. The mystical practices of Sufism have developed for over a thousand years from the experiences of thousands

Aswan High Dam and
Nile River, Egypt.

of Sufi masters. Sufi practices have adapted to the cultures and societies in which Sufism has been practiced, and Sufism has been practiced for centuries in Arabia, Iran, India, China, Indonesia, Africa, and Europe.

Although this chapter covers the basic principles and practices of Sufism, no one can do justice to the full range and richness of the Sufi tradition. In this chapter, we will be looking at Sufism primarily through a Sunni, Turkish Sufi lens.

The term *Sufi* has several root meanings in Arabic, including purity and wool. All Sufis seek outer and inner purity. The early Sufis wore rough, patched woolen cloaks instead of fancier clothing. Another meaning is row. At the time of the Prophet ﷺ, there was a group of devoted Muslims who sat in a row in front of his house in Madinah. They accompanied him whenever they could, and it is said that this group received esoteric instruction from the Prophet ﷺ and were the first Sufis.

There are several terms for those who practice Sufism. Besides the term *Sufi*, they are called dervishes, a Persian word related to door. A dervish stands at the threshold between the material and spiritual worlds, constantly seeking to enter more fully the spiritual realm. A third term is *faqir*, from the Arabic root, poverty. Poverty refers to the simple lifestyle practiced by the Sufis. Many early Sufis were wandering mendicants who relied on the charity of others for food and shelter. Another meaning is inner poverty, or lack of attachment to material possessions, and *faqir* also means dependent on, as in solely dependent on the power of the divine.

Most of the conventionally religious stop at the outer form of religious practice. They worship God and live a moral and ethical life, abiding by the teachings of their religion. For the mystics, outward practice is only a means toward unity with God.

FOUR LEVELS OF
SUFISM

Ibn Arabi is considered "the greatest sheikh," or teacher, in Sufism. He described four levels, or stages, of Sufi practice: *Shariah* (the religious law), *tariqa* (the mystical path), *haqiqa* (Truth), and *marifa* (Gnosis).

THE SHARIAH

The Shariah is the teachings and practices of Islam. In Arabic *shariah* means road. It is a clear path that anyone can follow. The Shariah teaches us how to live and act morally and ethically in the world. It teaches the outer forms of prayer and worship, forms learned by all Muslims. It is the foundation for Sufism. Trying to practice Sufism without the Shariah is like trying to build a house on a foundation of sand.

THE TARIQA

Second is the *tariqa*, the practice of Sufi discipline, designed for inner transformation. In Arabic *tariqa* refers to the way to proceed from oasis to oasis in the desert. It is not a clearly marked road or a visible path. You need a guide who knows the area intimately, or else you will become lost in the desert. The guide is the Sufi sheikh.

My Sufi master used to say the Shariah makes our outsides clean and attractive, and the *tariqa* makes our insides clean and pure. We need both on our spiritual journey.

HAQIQA

The third level is *haqiqa*. The Truth of Islam and of Sufism is the inner meaning of the practices and principles of the Shariah and *tariqa*. It is based on direct experience of the presence of God within. Until we reach this level of understanding, our practice is merely blind imitation. The development of *haqiqa* brings a whole new level of knowledge and sophistication to the religious and spiritual paths.

MARIFA

Fourth is *marifa*—deep wisdom and true knowledge of spirituality. This wisdom comes from the light of the soul, when it is fully uncovered within us. This is the level attained by the prophets and great saints.

Ibn Arabi explained that, at the level of Shariah, "there is yours and mine." That is, the Shariah teaches individual rights, and moral and ethical relations among people. At the level of *tariqa*, "what is mine is yours and what is yours is mine." The Sufis are brothers and sisters to each other, and they seek to open their hearts, their homes, and their hands to each other. This is powerful medicine to cure the possessiveness of the ego.

At the level of *haqiqa*, "there is no mine and no yours." This represents a whole new level of understanding, a realization that all things come from God, all things will return to God, and we are only caretakers and "possess" nothing. This realization brings about real independence from the world; we lose our attachment to money, fame, and material possessions. At the level of *marifa*, "there is no 'me' and no 'you'." The prophets and saints have realized all is God, and nothing is separate from God. They have attained Unity.

PATHS OF
SUFISM

There is no single path of Sufism. As the Prophet ﷺ said, "There are as many paths to God as there are souls." Some of the most common disciplines of Sufism are: devotion, service, remembrance, meditation, retreat, self-analysis, wisdom, self-discipline, and community. These disciplines are all interconnected, and each one supports the others.

DEVOTION

Sufism has been called the "path of the heart." Great Sufi poets have written eloquently of the soul's love and longing for God, the Beloved. My Sufi master described this love as follows:

> The eyes of the dervish who is a true lover see nought but God; his heart knows nought but Him. God is the eye by which he sees, the hand with which he holds, and

the tongue with which he speaks. . . .Were he not in love, he would pass away. If his heart should be devoid of love for as much as a single moment, the dervish could not stay alive. Love is the dervish's life, his health, his comfort. Love ruins the dervish, makes him weep; union makes him flourish, brings him to life. [4]

SERVICE

Service is the sister of devotion. As our hearts open with the love of God, we realize that all hearts yearn for God, and God is hidden in every heart. God placed a divine spark in our hearts and it is waiting to burst into flaming love and joy. If we realize that every heart contains God, then, as an essential aspect of our spiritual journey, we have to serve others.

One of the greatest services is to help heal the injured hearts of others. My Sufi master taught, "Every kind word or glance softens your heart, and every hurtful word or act closes or hardens your heart." To ignore God in the hearts of others is to separate ourselves from the union we so desire.

> If someone sits with me
> And we talk about the Beloved,
>
> If I cannot give his heart comfort,
> If I cannot make him feel better
> About himself and this world,
>
> Then, Hafiz,
> Quickly run to the mosque and pray—
> For you have just committed
> The only sin I know.   Hafiz [6]

Two Mevlevi dervishes bowing in respect to their sheikh, Konya, Turkey.

IBN SINA (AVICENNA), THE GREAT PHYSICIAN AND PHILOSOPHER

Ibn Sina (980–1037 C.E.) was born near Bukhara in Central Asia. Known in the West as Avicenna, he was the most famous physician, philosopher, encyclopedist, mathematician, and astronomer of his age. He was one of the greatest intellectual giants of all time. By the age of ten, Ibn Sina had memorized the Qur'an and had become well versed in the basic sciences. At 17, he cured the King of Bukhara of a serious illness after all the greatest physicians were called in and had given up hope.

At 20, Ibn Sina was already known as a learned man. He continued to study medicine throughout his life, working with thousands of patients in the free clinics he established. Ibn Sina's original contributions include descriptions of the contagious nature of tuberculosis, the spread of disease by water and soil, and the effects of psychology on health. He was the first to describe meningitis, and he also made major contributions to anatomy, gynecology, and child health.

Ibn Sina lived at the courts of many local rulers, including Isfahan, the capital of Persia, where he completed many of his monumental writings. Ibn Sina's major work was his five-volume Canon of Medicine, which summarized over one thousand years of history and traditions of medical practice. It is an immense encyclopedia of medicine comprised of over a million words.

The Canon was translated into Latin in the twelfth century, and it became the basic textbook for medical education in Europe until the seventeenth century. At the end of the fifteenth century 16 editions were published—15 editions in Latin and one in Hebrew. It was reissued more than 20 times during the sixteenth century. No discussion of the science of medicine can be complete without a reference to Ibn Sina.

Ibn Sina wrote an average of 50 pages a day and is the author of 238 books and monographs. His Book of Healing is a philosophical encyclopedia that covers everything from philosophy to science, and he wrote two other major works in philosophy as well. Ibn Sina also contributed to mathematics, physics, chemistry, zoology, botany, geology, psychology, theology, ethics, politics, mysticism, literature, music, and Qur'anic commentary. Known in the West as the "Prince of Physicians," Ibn Sina was more renowned in the East as a great philosopher. He is also considered to be the father of modern geology.

My Sufi teacher used to tell the following story about service.

Harun ar-Rashid was once walking through an orchard when he saw an old man planting date palms. He greeted him, and asked, "What are you doing, father?"

"As you see, I am planting date palms."

"How many years does it take a date palm to bear fruit?"

"Ten, twenty, thirty years. Some take as long as a hundred years."

"So you won't be able to eat the fruit of these palms you are planting."

"I may not live to see the day," said the old man, "but we eat from those trees our forefathers planted. So let us plant, that those who follow us may eat in turn!"

These words touched the caliph, and he tossed the old man a purse of gold coins.

The man took the purse, exclaiming, "I give praise to God, for the trees I planted here have borne fruit immediately!"

The caliph was so impressed by this that he gave him another purse of gold.

Said the old man, "I give praise to God! Trees normally bear fruit only once a year, but mine have produced two crops in one day!"

Throwing him yet another purse of gold, the caliph turned to his aide and said, "Quick, let us get away from here before this old man leaves us penniless."

A worshiper engaged in individual devotions after completing his formal prayer.

REMEMBRANCE

Remembrance of God fuels our devotion and service. The Sufis seek constant remembrance, never forgetting that we are in God's Presence, constantly feeling God within us. As God says in the Qur'an, "I am closer to you than your own jugular vein." Prayer is practice of remembrance, as are meditation, spiritual chanting, and spiritual study.

One basic Sufi spiritual practice is *Dhikrullah*, or Remembrance of God. This practice varies with different Sufi Orders, but it generally includes repetition of one or more of the 99 Divine Names. In many orders, Remembrance includes body movements, ranging from a simple movement of the head from right to left to the exquisite turning (called in the West, "whirling") of the Mevlevi dervishes. In some orders, repetition is done silently; in others, it is done aloud.

MEDITATION AND CONTEMPLATION

Meditation is another basic Sufi practice. There are many forms of meditation. Most common is introvert meditation in which the meditator remains still, seeking to quiet the mind and find God in the depths of that stillness. Sufis often practice extrovert meditation, in which chanting and repetitive movement focus mind and body on God.

Contemplation is another form of meditation. Sufis study verses of the Qur'an seeking their deeper meaning. All Muslims believe in studying the Qur'an. The Sufis seek to read two other Books as well—the Book of nature and the Book of one's life.

A Qur'anic verse is called an *ayah*, literally a sign. Each verse is a sign of God, and so is everything in nature—each tree, every sunset, the wind and rain, day and night, life and death. Contemplation of God's signs brings wisdom, and the Sufis are ideally reminded of God by everything around them. Their

"ONE HOUR OF CONTEMPLATION IS WORTH SIXTY YEARS OF WORSHIP." MUHAMMAD ﷺ [9]

world is permeated with God's presence. They experience the truth of the ayah, "Wherever you turn there is the Face of God" (2:115).

God also wrote the Book of our lives. Through self-analysis we can remove the veils that hide God's Presence from us. We can see how our egos and false imagination have kept us from seeing the Truth. Through contemplation we can also uncover God's Presence within us. Muhammad ﷺ taught, "Those who know themselves, know their Creator." [10]

A Westerner's Experience of *Dhikrullah*

" '*Hu-Allah, Hu-Allah*.' As my body responded to the rhythm, each syllable seemed to take on an existence of its own, as though the sound and I were one, a channel for the outpouring of some greater force. I felt the *Hu* ["Thou"] high in my throat, like a fragment of the ocean captured in a seashell; Allah reverberated in my heart, deep and forceful. I heard and felt the sounds, but they came forth effortlessly, as though I had tapped into a dimension that had always existed and allowed it to flow through me for an instant.

"The joy that I had first felt. ... gave way to a deep inner love, and to a conviction that there is indeed something beyond the mind; there is God; there is truly a source of all life. My fear was gone, leaving in its place a complete trust in the moment and in this old man beside me.

"He changed the chant to the single word "*Allah*.". . . The air inside my body was compressed down into the solar plexus and then up into the heart, exploding from my heart into the world on the second syllable of the word. The phenomenal world, my body, the amphitheater and the beach—even my own past had vanished, swallowed up in the Name. There was no future, there was just this moment." [8]

RETREAT

Retreat is a universal practice, a part of every spiritual tradition. The great saints and prophets practiced retreat; the best-known example is Moses' 40 days on Mount Sinai. Retreat is a time of silence and deep remembrance of God. A retreat can be as short as a day devoted to God alone, or it can be a classic 40-day Sufi retreat, modeled after Moses' time on Mount Sinai. The Prophet ﷺ taught, "Whoever devotes themselves solely to God for 40 days, fountains of wisdom shall pour from their hearts upon their tongues." [11]

Women gather at the Kraton, Jakarta, Indonesia, for prayers and to read the Qur'an during an Islamic holiday.

A European Muslim psychologist and dervish found that her 40-day retreat brought her an entirely new love of the Prophet ﷺ and a new closeness to the Qur'an.

Excerpts from *Forty Days: The Diary of a Traditional Solitary Sufi Retreat*

Day 10

It takes a while longer before the full extent of the miracle that has happened to me today becomes accessible to my conscious knowledge as well. I've often thought about one of the basic requirements of Islam: one must *love* the Prophet ﷺ. That always struck me as an impossibility. The way I understand "loving," it's a feeling that develops in the course of contact with another being on the basis of certain shared experiences. How can I feel love for somebody who lived so long ago, with whom I could never have had any contact? A command to show respect and deference towards the Prophet ﷺ would have seemed appropriate to me. But love? My intense involvement with the historical Muhammad ﷺ had indeed taught me the greatest admiration for this extraordinary person. . . . But the Islamic command to love him, a person long since dead, struck me as impossible, illogical, unthinkable.

   Only now do I see how correct the word "unthinkable" is for this command. Of course love isn't something that could ever be achieved by thinking, by an effort of the will. When it "hits," that is pure grace. Could that be what is meant when my Teacher is always talking about "going through the heart"? Understanding what that means is still impossible for me. But all at once I have been allowed to have the direct, living experience of the "unthinkable." ...

Day 37

I know with greater and greater certainty what I don't want to do: reading or any other purely cognitive activities. I have such a craving for the direct closeness that only becomes accessible through intuitive approaches. Yearning for the way of the heart. Only how? All I can give is my defective *zhikrs*. The result is in other hands. I can't do anything but make an honest effort.

Reading the Qur'an ... is something that amazes me. Besides the eight surahs that the sheikh "prescribed" for me, I had planned to read the entire Qur'an. Doing it all in sequence is something I have done only once before in my life, as a 13-year-old. At that time I was beginning to get interested in the religion of the country where I grew up [Turkey]. Looking back, I can only say that it was mostly attributable to my persistence that I actually read the whole Qur'an through from beginning to end. As reading matter I simply found it boring and redundant.

Two decades later, when I had become a Muslim, I began to feel awe for the Holy Book but precisely because it is the Holy Book. It had little to do with the contents. ... Now, however, and it amazes me, my desire to read the Qur'an gets stronger every day. Indeed, it has become a craving instead of a dutiful exercise!

Partly, no doubt, that is because I am slowly penetrating more deeply into the multilayeredness of the contents. By no way is it that alone. People always mention the magical power that the Holy Book has in the original Arabic, which of necessity gets lost in the translations. Of course no translation

can ever be "authorized" in the religious sense. Despite all that, I am starting to feel this magic very clearly! It's almost irresistible. The book has a direct influence on my spirits, like some kind of magic spell! By now I also have three "favorite surahs," 48, 93, and 94, that I keep reading over and over. Reading the Qur'an isn't something cognitive anymore, it's a direct opening on an intuitive level.

The Second Day [After The 40-Day Retreat]

All of a sudden Muhammad ﷺ is with me again. Again this overwhelming presence strikes right to my heart, again there are tears upon tears, and finally tears of joy again. How could I ever be so dumb, how could I have doubted again, after everything that I now *know*? How could I have been so blind that I still didn't see the hand that holds the pen? Not to realize that so many of my prayers had been answered at once? It isn't God's way to deal with each problem separately and by itself: *one* answer clarifies all questions and the difficulty is solved. ...

How I had prayed that ... after the *halvet* [retreat] my "inner *halvet*" might continue! And that I might be given an opportunity to be of service by passing love and selflessness along! That my pain if necessary might persist until I "remembered" for certain. ...

What unexpected riches I have been given just when I least expected them! And at the same time I also have the direct experiential knowledge that I have not been abandoned, that the blessing of the *halvet* continues wherever I may be! *Wherever you turn, there is Allah's face* (Qur'an 2:115). ...

For a long time I just lie there feeling the grace of deepest, most selfless love flooding through me, wave upon wave. [12]

COMMUNITY

Sufi groups are like families. The teacher or sheikh is the parent, and the dervishes are brothers and sisters. Instead of the sibling rivalry and poor parenting common in many real families, a Sufi community provides an opportunity to practice and experience patience, loving compassion, and service. Our brother and sister dervishes are mirrors that show us ourselves. We can learn to be patient with our own weaknesses when we see them in others, and we can also learn to focus more on each other's strengths and beauties, and less on each other's weaknesses.

Dervishes often think of each other as companions on a difficult and demanding journey. A man came to a famous sheikh and asked, "True companions are scarce in these times. Where am I to find a companion in God?" The sheikh replied, "If you want a companion to provide for you and to bear your burden, such are few and far between. However, if you want a companion in God whose burden you will carry and whose pain you will bear, then I have a multitude I can introduce you to." 13

One of the cornerstones of Sufi practice is the imitation of the Prophet ﷺ. Muhammad ﷺ is considered a perfect human being, the best possible role model. In striving to be more like him, Sufis cultivate patience, generosity, respect, kindness, devotion, and commitment to spiritual practice. They also strive to rid themselves of negative traits such as pride, greed, egotism, and other faults. The *hadith* opposite is an excellent guide for the Sufis.

Working to transform oneself is known as the inner *jihad*, or inner struggle. The Qur'an often uses the term *jihad* in the context of struggle in the way of God. In a famous *hadith*, Muhammad ﷺ was riding back to Madinah after the battle of Badr when he commented, "Now we are going to the greater *jihad*!" The warriors were exhausted and could not imagine fighting another battle. The Prophet ﷺ went on, "The greater *jihad* is the struggle with what is in your breast."

A Sufi celebration, Bitshah, Pakistan.

foster balance and health, preventing illness. Similarly the practices of Sufism will bring us to a healthy spiritual balance so that our inner wisdom and spiritual nature can blossom naturally. A sheikh knows what practices to prescribe for each student to help that student develop spiritually.

Why is a sheikh, or guide, necessary? A guide is someone who has explored his or her own inner nature and is capable of leading others to explore their own inner spiritual depths. A sheikh teaches from experience, as the following story illustrates:

Nasruddin, a Sufi teacher, was serving as a local judge. A woman came to him with her son and complained that her son had an uncontrollable sweet tooth. She asked Nasruddin to tell the boy to stop eating sweets all the time. Nasruddin agreed and told her to come back in two weeks. When they returned, he said simply, "Young man, stop eating sweets! It is no good for you."

The mother asked, "Why did you have us wait for two weeks? Couldn't you have said this to my son when we first came to you?"

Nasruddin replied, "No, I couldn't possibly have told that to your son two weeks ago. First, I had to stop eating sweets!"

This story only seems funny because we are used to learning facts and talking about them without living by what we have learned. One of the requirements of a sheikh is to practice what he or she teaches. Empty words help no one.

According to an old Turkish saying, we can put a bandage on a cut, but we cannot operate on ourselves. Similarly, we can engage in a certain amount of self-reflection and self-discipline by ourselves, but for major transformation, we need the help, support, and advice of a guide. By definition, we can only operate within our current

AYAZ AND THE GOBLET

Sultan Mahmud of Ghazna was sitting at dinner with his closest advisors. Everyone admired his magnificent crystal goblet, one of his greatest treasures. The sultan handed the goblet to his grand wazir (chief minister) and said, "Break it!" The wazir replied, "I could not, my sultan. It is too precious, and I would not dare to destroy one of your most valuable treasures."

The sultan handed the goblet to each of his advisors with the same instructions, and each refused to break the magnificent goblet. Finally, he handed the goblet to Ayaz. When he told Ayaz to break the goblet, Ayaz immediately smashed it to pieces. The others were amazed and annoyed.

The sultan asked Ayaz why he broke the goblet, and Ayaz replied, "My sultan, I knew that the goblet was very precious, but far more precious to me is your command. I would not dream of refusing your wishes, and so I immediately did what you told me to do."

The sultan turned to the others and said, "You see why I love and trust him." Ideally, the dervish has the same love and obedience toward the sheikh.

limits; outside help is essential to transcend our boundaries and achieve real transformation.

The most important function of a sheikh is to provide an atmosphere of love and trust for each dervish. The sheikh's unconditional love and trust in the dervish's capacity for spiritual growth are essential foundations for Sufi practice. In this atmosphere, the dervishes begin to heal their hearts of the pain and wounds experienced in this world. They gain the confidence to undergo the rigors of transformation and develop the belief in their capacity for spiritual growth and their worthiness to seek and find God.

God is the ocean, the sheikh is a river leading to the ocean, and the dervish is a drop of water. The drop becomes one with the river and eventually one with the ocean. This union is accomplished through remembrance.

SUFI
POETRY

The dervish's love and longing for God are most beautifully expressed by the great Sufi poets. Read the following selections slowly. Allow them to touch your heart, to contact your own longing for God. The following lines are from the opening of Rumi's greatest work, the Mathnawi:

> Listen to the reed flute, crying of separation.
> "Ever since I was plucked from the reed bed,
> men and women have wept along with my grieving cries.
> I want a torn heart, torn from separation,
> a heart that understands the sweet pain of yearning for
>   union." Rumi [16]

We are that flute, taken from our spiritual home and forced to endure the separation of life in this world. It is God's breath that blows through us, creating our lament for reunion with God.

Rumi also reminds us of the importance of waking up and becoming more conscious:

Far right: Dawn over the rooftops and minarets of Istanbul, Turkey.

The reeds growing in their reed bed.

> The breeze at dawn has secrets to tell you.
> Don't go back to sleep.
> You must ask for what you really want.
> Don't go back to sleep.
> People are going back and forth across the doorsill
> Where the two worlds touch.
> The door is round and open.
> Don't go back to sleep. [17]

We all suffer from the sleep of heedlessness. We think we are awake, but we suffer from "waking sleep." The goal of Sufism is to wake up, find the doorway between heaven and earth, and enter.

> Today, like every other day, we wake up empty and frightened.
> Don't open the door to the study and begin reading.
> Take down a musical instrument.
> Let the beauty we love be what we do.
> There are hundreds of ways to kneel and kiss the ground. [18]

Until we find God, we wake up every day frightened and empty. We distract ourselves to disguise the emptiness. We kneel and touch the ground five times a day in prayer, but how often do we pray while distracted, our hearts still seeking worldly goals? Love will bring us to God, more quickly than anything else.

> No better love than love with no object,
> no more satisfying work than work with no purpose.
> If you could give up tricks and cleverness,
> that would be the cleverest trick! [19]

Gamble everything for love,
if you're a true human being.

If not, leave this gathering.

Half-heartedness doesn't reach into majesty.
You set out to find God,
but then you keep stopping for long periods
at mean-spirited roadhouses. [20]

If the beloved is everywhere,
the lover is a veil,

but when living itself becomes
the Friend, lovers disappear. [21]

I rarely let the word "No" escape
From my mouth
Because it is so plain to my soul
That God has shouted, "Yes! Yes! Yes!" [22]

OMAR KHAYYAM: POET AND SCIENTIST

Omar Khayyam (1048–1131) was a respected mathematician and astronomer as well as a great Persian poet. He was in charge of an observatory in Persia, and devised a new calendar that was so accurate, it was out by only one day in five thousand years! His Rubaiyat (verse) has become famous throughout the Western world.

> Awake! For morning in the bowl of night
> has flung the stone that puts the stars to flight:
> And lo! The hunter of the east has caught
> the sultan's turret in a noose of light.

Here with a loaf of bread beneath the bough,
a flask of wine, a book of verse—and thou
beside me singing in the wilderness
and wilderness is paradise enough.

The moving finger writes; and, having writ,
moves on: nor all thy piety nor wit
shall lure it back to cancel half a line,
nor all thy tears wash out a word of it.

(Rubaiyat, 1, 11, 51)

EXPERIENCE ISLAM

REMEMBRANCE OF GOD

One of the most important Sufi practices is to remember God through repetition of a holy phrase or one of the Names of God. One hundred times a day, repeat the phrase *La ilaha ilAllah*, "There are no gods, there is God." Keep track of the number of repetitions by using prayer beads, a mechanical counter, or by counting on your fingers.

As you recite *La ilaha*, turn your head to the right, and when you recite *ilAllah*, turn your head to the left and slightly downward, toward your heart. My Sufi master used to say that the heart is a divine temple. With each repetition of *La ilaha*, you clean out the temple, removing the dust and the idols of worldly attachments, and making the heart temple more suitable for God's Presence. With each repetition of *ilAllah*, you sanctify the heart temple.

Sit in a quiet place where there are no distractions. Take your time and focus on the meaning of the words you recite. You can practice either by reciting aloud or silently. Try to feel the practice deepen. We all begin with remembrance of the tongue, or mechanical repetition of the words. This descends to remembrance of the heart, in which the phrase comes alive within us and opens our hearts. Finally, remembrance descends to the remembrance of the soul. The remembrance connects us to the divine within ourselves, the divine soul that has always been and always will be in communion with God.

It is said that sincere repetition of this phrase can bring about such a deep and powerful inner cleansing that all our past sins are forgiven.

OPENING YOUR HEART

There are many powerful Sufi practices designed to open the heart. Try one of the following practices. Stay with it until you feel your heart begin to open, and then continue to stay with the practice until you sense that your change of heart has become solid and stable.

A Bedtime Prayer Before going to bed, say silently in your heart three times, "God is with me. God beholds me. God watches over me." In time increase this to seven, then eleven times.

When he was three years old, a Sufi sheikh was taught this prayer by his uncle. After he repeated the prayer three times a night for several nights, his uncle told him to say it seven times, then eleven. He reported that he felt a sweetness growing in his heart. His uncle told him to keep up the prayer as it would help him in this world and in the next. The sheikh reported, "After several years, I found an ever-deepening sweetness within myself."

A Heart Prayer The Prophet ﷺ taught this prayer to his companions: "O God, grant me love of You and to love those who love You and to love whatever brings me nearer to You. O God, make Your love more precious to me than cool water to the thirsty."

An Illuminated Heart The divine light of the soul is contained within the heart. Mentally remove the veils that hide this light and let your heart radiate light to everyone and everything you meet. Feel that you have a miniature divine sun in your chest. Let the light of your heart touch and warm the hearts of those around you. No matter who they are or what their personality is like, their heart yearns for God, just as yours does.

ADAB, RIGHT ACTION

The root of *adab* is "to invite guests, or to gather people together for a banquet." It refers to the basic Islamic values of generosity, good hospitality, and service to others. To have good *adab* is to think of others' needs instead of thinking only of oneself. For example, I have been in Islamic households in which the host and hostess served the guests first and only ate after all their guests were fed. During the meal they devoted themselves completely to the needs of their guests.

If service alone was enough, every waiter and waitress would be a saint. However, for many people service is either a duty or a way of earning money. Good *adab* is to serve out of genuine desire to help others, not for any personal gain. According to an old Sufi saying, "A real sheikh never visits a sultan. Even if the sheikh is in the palace, the sultan is his guest." That is, a real sheikh wants only to serve the sultan, not to get anything from him.

I have learned much about *adab* from the old dervishes. When one dervish serves another tea, *adab* turns this simple event into something profound. The server is aware that it is an honor and a privilege to serve another human being. The one being served realizes that she is being given a real gift from the heart. Both are conscious; both are grateful.

Keep an "*adab* journal." Every evening review your day and write down the ways you served others. Note ways in which your *adab* might improve, and make intention to serve in new or better ways for the next day. In a famous *hadith*, the Prophet ﷺ said, "I was sent to teach *adab*."

Reciting the Names of God using prayer beads.

THE MIND
OF ISLAM

According to Islamic psychology,[1] human nature
is composed of two basic elements: our material
nature and our spiritual nature. Our material
nature is composed of body, mind, and ego. Our
spiritual nature consists of heart and soul. In
addition, Islamic psychology distinguishes six
stations of human beings. These stations are based
on a person's spiritual level of attainment. They
are the Prophets, the Saints, the Believers, the
Religious, the Worldly, and the Deniers of faith.

The West readily imported Islamic contributions to science, mathematics, and medicine, yet Islamic psychology is still virtually unknown to Western scholars. The main contributions to Islamic psychology have been made by the Sufi masters, who have drawn on an unbroken, thousand-year-old tradition of spiritual and psychological guidance. Because Sufism is far more closely tied to Islam than medicine, mathematics, or science, it has had less impact on Western thought.

The following analysis of human nature and the stations of humanity comes primarily from concepts and descriptions commonly used by Muslims. Although the six stages do not appear in exactly the same form in traditional texts, these concepts are familiar to all Muslims and are rooted in the Qur'an. In addition, I have added my own analysis and interpretation based on over 20 years of observation of Muslim psychology. The five aspects and six stations describe how Muslims view the world, as well as unconscious beliefs and assumptions that affect Muslim thought and behavior. The patterns described here are patterns both of and for Muslim behavior.

By patterns of behavior I mean observable regularities in thought or action. By patterns for behavior I mean a description of behavior that may represent an ideal pattern or a conscious or unconscious prescriptive set of cultural and psychospiritual expectations.

"GOD LIKES GENEROSITY AND FORGIVENESS, AND DISLIKES AN ILL TEMPER AND JEALOUSY."

MUHAMMAD ﷺ 3

FIVE ASPECTS OF HUMAN NATURE

Much of our behavior is based on the drives and needs of the body. The mind, rooted in the brain, is implanted in the body. The ego results from the development of the concept of self plus identification with mind and body instead of heart and soul. These three elements make up our material nature.

The soul, or *ruh*, is located in our heart of hearts, and our heart and soul make up our spiritual nature. By heart, I mean the spiritual heart, or *qalb* in Arabic. It is the seat of love, compassion, and intuitive intelligence. Rumi calls our two intellects the "acquired intellect" and the "complete intellect." The "acquired intellect," of the head, is based on learning from outside sources. The heart knows from within.

In a healthy individual, the material and spiritual aspects are balanced and integrated. The two aspects are deeply intertwined; all our thoughts and actions combine the spiritual and the material. A body without spirit is a corpse, and a soul without a body is a ghost. Unfortunately, our society tends to emphasize the material to the extent that it leads to imbalance in most people. Islamic psychology emphasizes the need for balance, which means to nourish the spiritual.

According to the Qur'an, all human beings are created from a single original essence. That original pattern, or genetic disposition, is innate in each one of us, a basic nature inherent in all human beings.

This innate nature is called, in Arabic, *fitra* (the natural disposition of the self), or a healthy self. In a well-known *hadith*, the Prophet ﷺ said that every child is born with an intact, healthy self and is in submission to the Truth. But body and the environment—especially, culture and society—interfere and influence us in other directions.

Material	Body	Animal nature	Lower emotions—anger, fear, lust
	Mind	Mental nature	Worldly thinking—dominated by materialism
	Ego	Separatist nature	Narcissism, desire for praise and recognition
Spiritual	Heart	Human nature	Higher emotions—compassion, love
			Higher thinking—creativity, intuition
	Soul	Divine nature	Infinite Divine light and wisdom

1 Body Our bodies are the seat of our animal nature, or *ruh haywani*. We share many characteristics with the animal kingdom, as our physical bodies are basically the same as the bodies of other mammals, with the exception of a more developed brain and nervous system. We experience hunger, thirst, sexual desire, and emotions such as anger and fear—just as animals do. Often enough, our behavior is driven primarily by the tendencies of our animal nature.

When we feel "possessed" by anger or "overcome" with desire, it is a clear sign we are behaving in accordance with our animal nature. In fact, it is a sign that our animal nature has managed to dominate the other aspects of our personality. Our animal nature is composed of bodily drives and needs. Obviously a healthy animal nature helps us maintain a healthy body. Without hunger or thirst, we would become undernourished and unhealthy, and without a sex drive there would be no new generation. The main problem with our animal nature is the possibility of imbalance—many people end up devoting most of their lives to the body's needs and desires.

2 Mind The development of the brain brings the ability for more complex thinking and deeper understanding of the world around us. Human beings have better memories than animals and greater abilities to cope with their environment.

We have developed language, an incredibly powerful tool for communication and for the creation of mental models of the world. Just as a healthy animal nature leads to a healthy body, a healthy mental nature leads to a healthier life. We also create mental models of ourselves. We develop an ego, which allows us to represent ourselves in relation to our environment.

A young Muslim girl, Tehran, Iran.

Muslims beginning to gather at the mosque before the time of prayer.

3 Ego In Arabic the ego is called the *nafs*. The lowest level of the *nafs* is the narcissistic ego. To the extent we identify with the mind and body and not the soul, we develop a series of tendencies that hide or distort the light and wisdom of the soul. The first and most harmful development is the development of a sense of separateness, which is one of the basic characteristics of the narcissistic ego. God is Unity, and the truth of the universe is unity. As we think of ourselves as separate, we separate ourselves from the rest of Creation and from God, and also from our own souls. We develop egotism or narcissism, the tendency to think only of ourselves, to act only in ways that benefit ourselves.

"BE HUMBLE, SINCE HUMILITY IS IN THE HEART." MUHAMMAD ﷺ 4

Narcissists are aware only of their own needs. They put themselves first and everyone else second. They even put themselves before God, and so the narcissistic ego is directly opposed to our spiritual nature. The narcissistic ego contains all those tendencies that conflict with our spiritual nature. This includes identification with the desires of the body—for example, being run by our sexual desires. It includes the ego's need for constant praise and gratification.

4 Heart Only when the spiritual heart opens do we become fully human. According to Islamic psychology, our human nature, or *ruh insani*, is essentially spiritual. The soul is located in the depths of our hearts, and when the heart opens, the wisdom and intuition of the soul shine forth. As the heart opens, we begin to see with the eyes of the heart, to hear with the ears of the heart, and to understand with the intelligence of the heart.

With the opening of the heart we develop our capacity to love and to feel compassion for others. Faith develops at this stage, as we come in touch with our own spiritual nature. In a famous *hadith qudsi*, God says, "The heavens and the earth cannot contain Me, yet I fit into the heart of the sincere believer." My Sufi master used to teach that it is worse to break a single heart than to destroy the Ka'bah in Makkah or any other holy temple. These temples were built by human beings to worship God, but the heart was built by God to house God.

The heart is the seat of real creativity and true understanding. The most creative and successful people are those who are the most passionate about their work. The mind is limited, a function of the physical nervous system. It is like a computer that can store and manipulate information. The computer can make new combinations of information, but it is not capable of generating new ideas. Our creative intelligence is rooted in the heart.

The heart is the battleground of the conflicting tendencies of our material and spiritual natures. To the extent we favor our material tendencies, our hearts become filled with the love of things of this world, and there is no room left for love of God. These material attachments become veils that hide our souls and obscure our spiritual natures. As we reduce these attachments, our hearts become lighter and our inner spiritual nature becomes more apparent.

Become a person of the heart
or at least the devotee of one;
Or else, you will remain
like a donkey stuck in the mud.
If one has no heart,
one can gain no benefit;
In wretchedness, one
will be famous in the world. Rumi [7]

5 Soul According to the Qur'an, the human race began when God breathed a soul from God's own soul into Adam and then into Eve. We originated with the combination of our material bodies and our transcendent spiritual nature. Our souls are sparks of the divine, transmitted to us directly from God.

The soul remains unaffected by the world. It is like a light hidden under a basket. Even if it is completely hidden, the light itself is unchanged.

Our soul is in constant prayer, constant remembrance of God. This divine spark in us is infinitely larger than all material creation because it retains the infinite nature of its divine source. As God is infinite, every spark of God is infinite as well.

IBN KHALDUN

One of the foremost thinkers in Islamic history was the great historian and philosopher Ibn Khaldun (1332–1406). His masterpiece, An Introduction to History, is considered the first major scientific study of history and sociology.

Ibn Khaldun was born in Tunis and was educated in Tunis and Fez. He studied the Qur'an and other branches of Islamic studies as well as Arabic literature, philosophy, mathematics and astronomy. He is best known for his Introduction, the first volume of his world history, a brilliant exposition of philosophy of history and sociology. Ibn Khaldun emphasized the need to subject both social and historical phenomena to scientific and objective analysis. He noted that these phenomena were not the outcome of chance but were controlled by laws of their own.

Ibn Khaldun has been a major influence in history, philosophy of history, sociology, political science, and education. He was also a pioneer in the art of autobiography and an inspiration in the fields of education, educational psychology, and Arabic prose.

Ibn Khaldun: An Appreciation, by Murad Hoffman

Those who still believe that it is in the nature of Islam to impede progress would do themselves a favor if they read ... the introductory book of Ibn Khaldun's monumental world history ... written in 1377. ... If Ibn Khaldun, supreme judge (qadi) in Cairo, had produced no more than those 1,400 introductory pages, he would have made intellectual history. As it is, 500 years before Karl Marx and Max Weber, he became the real father of both sociology and the philosophy of history, requiring history to be "more than just information."

Ibn Khaldun made the earliest known attempt to discover the laws that govern historical cycles and the rise and fall of civilizations, and to write history after submitting traditional source materials to an impartial, critical, even skeptical scrutiny. This approach led Ibn Khaldun to study the interaction between climate and behavior, and between urban specialization and cultural traits. ...

But let us not forget: Ibn Khaldun was neither an exceptional genius nor an aberration. He was a product of Islamic culture at its best. [6]

"DEAR FRIEND, YOUR HEART IS A POLISHED MIRROR. YOU MUST WIPE IT CLEAN OF THE VEIL OF DUST THAT HAS GATHERED UPON IT, BECAUSE IT IS DESTINED TO REFLECT THE LIGHT OF DIVINE SECRETS." ABD AL-QADIR AL-JILANI [5]

STATIONS OF HUMANITY

Islamic psychology distinguishes six stations of human beings. Each station represents a different way of being in the world and relating to God. Each station portrays a different degree of access to the soul and a different balance between our material and spiritual natures.

In Arabic the word for station is *maqam*, which also means a musical mode, like a major or minor key. An infinite number of melodies can be played in a minor key, but they all share certain basic characteristics. Similarly, people at a given station may have widely different personalities and backgrounds, but they all share certain basic characteristics. For example, all the prophets experience the highest levels of faith, purity, and love of God.

1 The Prophets The prophets occupy the highest station of humanity. God chose them to convey the Divine Message to the rest of humanity. It is revealed in the Qur'an that "every nation (i.e., community or tribe) has (been sent) an apostle." [10:47] According to Qur'anic commentators, there have been 124,000 prophets, who have taught, from time immemorial, every people, every nation and tribe on earth. A glass that is perfectly transparent and absolutely clean will allow light to pass through it undistorted; similarly, the prophets' inner and outer purity allowed them to transmit undistorted Divine Truth.

In their lives, the prophets embodied the Truths that they taught. They were worthy of teaching Truth because they lived the Truth. Some years after Muhammad's ﷺ passing, a group of Muslims came to his widow Aishah and requested her to tell them what he was like. She asked her visitors, "Have you read the Qur'an?" They replied, "Yes." She went on, "He was the living Qur'an."

Some prophets became world famous; others remained obscure. Some have millions of followers today; others may have had only one or two disciples in their lifetimes. But these differences are superficial. From an Islamic point of view, all the

1 Prophets	(*Nabi-ullah*)	Revealers of Divine Truth	Servants of God	Pure *nafs*
2 Saints	(*Wali-ullah*)	Interpreters of revealed Truth	Friends of God	Pleasing *nafs*
				Pleased nafs
3 Believers	(*Mumin*)	Spiritual greater than Material	Seekers of God	Serene *nafs*
4 Religious	(*Muslim*)	Spiritual equal to Material	Inner *jihad*	Inspired *nafs*
5 Worldly	(*Dunyayi*)	Material greater than Spiritual	Worldly focus	Regretful *nafs*
6 Deniers	(*Kafir*)	Spiritual is hidden	Deny spirituality	Tyrannical *nafs*

prophets are the same. They teach the same Truth from the same divine source. The same divine light of prophecy flowed, unobstructed and undistorted, through all of them.

According to Islam, the prophets were all servants of God. Just as sincere servants dedicate themselves to promoting their masters' interests, the prophets thought only of following God's Will. There was nothing in them that obstructed God's Will working freely through them. They controlled their egos, so their egos became their servants and not their masters. The prophets were at the stage of the pure self; they were able to "drop" their egos in order to reveal Divine Truth, undistorted.

They are not themselves, but insofar as they exist at all, they exist in God. Their movements are caused by God, and their words are the words of God uttered by their tongues, and their sight is the sight of God, which has entered into their eyes. So God Most High has said, "When I love a servant, I, the Lord, am his ear so that he hears by Me, I am his eye so that he sees by Me, and I am his tongue so that he speaks by Me, and I am his hand so that he takes by Me."

Dhu-l-Nun [8]

The border along the upper walls of this mosque repeats the phrase, "Victory belongs to God alone."

THE SAINT AND THE SULTAN

An old Sufi story illustrates the saints' attachment to God and their nonattachment to the world. When the sultan was parading through town, everyone bowed down to him except a Sufi saint who sat quietly, repeating the Names of God on his prayer beads. The sultan stopped the procession, offended that the Sufi paid no attention to him. When his guards brought the saint to the sultan, the saint explained, "It is right that all your people bow down to you, because they want what you have and they are afraid of what you might do to them. But I am afraid of God alone, and I only want whatever God chooses to give to me. So it is only right that I did not bow to you."

The saint went on, "Besides, it wouldn't be right for a free man to bow to a slave." Hearing this the sultan turned white with rage. His guards reached for their scimitars. The saint continued, unperturbed, "You have two masters that I conquered. You are still a slave to your pride and greed, but I mastered them long ago."

The sultan waved his guards away, saying, "Leave him alone. He is one of God's subjects, not one of mine."

The Qur'an refers to Muhammad ﷺ as the "seal" of the prophets. Once the seal is placed on an official document, nothing can be added. One of the most basic beliefs in Islam is that Muhammad ﷺ was the last prophet. One argument for this is that the Qur'an has been preserved intact, and with this complete Book, there is no need for additional revelations of God's Truth.

2 The Saints The lives of the saints are filled with the miracles and deep faith typical of the prophets. However, instead of bringing God's Message to Earth, the duty of the saints is to interpret the Truth that has been handed down by the prophets. They clarify the Truth in words and actions that fit their society and time in history. As living examples of

A girl practices her Arabic calligraphy at the Arab Culture Festival, Brooklyn, New York.

faith and charity, they renew the Truth in each generation. Without the example and the inner understanding of the saints, the Truth would inevitably become distorted or lost in the hands of the selfish, egotistical, and worldly.

As Rumi beautifully illustrates, the saints follow their divine nature and refuse to be run by the planning and scheming of their egos:

Do you think I know what I'm doing?
That for one breath or half-breath I belong to myself?
As much as a pen knows what it's writing,
or the ball can guess where it's going next. [9]

Like the prophets, the saints are motivated by their spiritual natures, and there is no real struggle with their material tendencies. However, material tendencies may slightly distort or inhibit the light and wisdom of the soul. The saints may slip from time to time into identification with body, mind, or ego; the prophets never forgot their divine nature. That is, all the prophets attained the state of the

The worldly are materialists who devote themselves to satisfying the needs and drives of body, mind, and ego. They are convinced that these needs are real and that spiritual needs are unreal and unimportant or, at best, take second place. Like someone with a long-standing vitamin deficiency, they are suffering from spiritual malnourishment, but they do not know it. The worldly may even go to the mosque once a week, but this momentary involvement with religion does not affect the rest of their lives. Prayer and other religious pursuits tend to be done more for social approval than for their spiritual significance.

Modern Western culture is basically a worldly culture. The values and behavior constantly depicted in the Western media are almost exclusively focused on material goals and pleasures. Spiritual aspirations are rarely mentioned or given any value or importance. If you have any doubt about this, look at our popular films and TV programs. Spiritual issues are rarely addressed, and the lives of the characters generally revolve around seeking money, fame, and sexual gratification. Our commercials are even worse examples of this.

For Muslims who are struggling with their own material desires, Western culture may seem like an enemy of all things religious. Those who are more grounded in their own spirituality try to integrate the positive aspects of Western culture with their spiritual lives. My Sufi master once said, "If you put the world between you and God, the world becomes a spiritual obstacle; if you use the world to remember God, the world becomes your spiritual friend."

The worldly are so used to being dominated by the desires of their egos that they mistake spiritual discipline for loss of freedom. They think they are free, but they are really prisoners of their egos and their animal nature's desires and impulses.

When my Sufi master visited Paris, France, with a group of dervishes, they had a French guide who became devoted to the sheikh and the dervishes. He was a sincere young man, liked by everyone. Toward the end of the visit, he inquired about becoming a dervish. The sheikh indicated he would be willing to consider initiating the young man. Then, the man asked, "but what about my freedom, *ma liberté?*" The sheikh slowly turned his back on the young man and walked away from him. As he left the room the sheikh said, "Let him keep his precious freedom!" The dervishes present said they never forgot this scene.

6 The Deniers of Faith Not only are the deniers' lives dominated by material concerns, they have actively repudiated the spiritual. They deny the existence of God and the reality of the spiritual. Their lives are dominated by the desires of their egos and the impulses of their bodies. They function mainly at the level of the tyrannical *nafs.*

The Arabic term for those who do not believe in God is *kafir,* from the verb *kaffara,* to hide or cover.

Window shopping, Kuwait. In most Muslim societies today, the traditional and the modern exist side by side.

"WHOEVER TRAVELS WITHOUT A GUIDE NEEDS TWO HUNDRED YEARS FOR A TWO-DAY JOURNEY." RUMI [13]

It refers to those people who have so covered the light of their own souls that they have no experience of their own spiritual nature, and they deny the reality of God and the truth of religion. Although *kafir* is often translated as nonbeliever, there is actually no word for nonbeliever in Arabic.

There are *kafir* cultures that seek to deny spirituality in all their members. If Western culture is worldly, Communist culture is *kafir*; it actively denies the truth of religion.

Most people at this stage are dominated by their tyrannical *nafs* and act only in their own self-interest. They are narcissists who think only of their own gain, and who are incapable of real compassion or caring for others. They will not forgo their needs for anyone or anything outside themselves. They refuse to recognize any higher authority or principles that might limit their self-seeking behavior. They only follow the rules of society from fear of punishment. They will break the law whenever they can get away with it, or they will try and distort the law and "bend" it in their favor.

Some people may call themselves atheists, but have dedicated their lives to service or to the search for Truth. In so doing, they live their lives in accordance with the underlying wisdom of all religions. Others may call themselves religious but actually have little or no faith.

Some believers make enemies of the deniers, criticizing their worldliness as sinful or evil. They are acting out the material desires that the religious are struggling with in themselves. Some *kafirs* look on all people of faith as confused, unrealistic dreamers, projecting onto others their own unresolved issues with their spiritual nature.

To call others *kafir* if they disagree with one's religious viewpoint is all too common among some Muslim bigots (and among bigots of other faiths as well). This generally occurs among the religious, who, in their own inner struggles between their material and spiritual natures, may project onto others their own inner doubts and their own unconscious antireligious tendencies.

Muhammad ﷺ insisted that no one is to label another a *kafir*. Only God knows our inner state. Only God knows whose prayers are acceptable. The Prophet ﷺ admonished, "Anyone who calls another a *kafir*, is himself or herself a *kafir*."

CONCLUSIONS

All religions are founded on the prophets' true communion with God. The experience of the great prophets is qualitatively different from the inner life of the average person. Worldly materialists may insist on projecting their own inner limitations onto the great spiritual teachers, but this only reflects their own profound lack of understanding of the potentials of human development.

It is beneficial to find a real spiritual teacher; there do exist those, at higher levels of development, who have greater understanding of spiritual truths because their inner wisdom is less veiled. In addition, all sincere seekers should study the lives and writings of prophets and saints; they are the best role models because they are the best of humanity and have a greater capacity to understand both the spirit and religious teachings. The actions and teachings of Muhammad ﷺ are taken as fully authorative because they reflect the divine light and wisdom which flowed through him.

EXPERIENCE ISLAM

YOUR MATERIAL AND SPIRITUAL NATURES

Set aside two chairs, one for your material and one for your spiritual side. When you sit in one chair, let your material side speak up, and when you sit in the other chair, let your spiritual side express itself. Allow your material and spiritual natures to dialogue. Let each part of yourself express its hopes, fears, and desires. Switch chairs as these two sides engage in dialogue. You might be surprised at what these two sides have to say to each other.

See if you can get these two sides to agree to work together instead of fighting with each other. You might want to tape-record the conversation so that you can review it later.

REMEMBERING GOD

Medicine for the believers is anything that reminds us of God. Try to occupy your thoughts with remembrance of God and your heart with the love of God. Occupy your spare moments with the poetry of the saints, reading and memorizing scripture, listening to hymns and other devotional music dedicated to God. Keep a devotional tape in your car and play it whenever driving. Keep an inspirational book by your bedside and read it before going to sleep. Find your own creative ways to remind yourself of God and to open your heart. You are always in God's presence.

GOD WITHIN

To develop deep inner peace, begin by calming your mind for just five to ten minutes. Do this with absolute faith that God is fully present within you, even if you are unaware of that presence. Practice with a sense of certainty and determination to realize God.

This is known in Zen as sitting with a "bright mind." It is extremely important to sit with the faith that your deepest nature is divine, that you need not add anything or develop anything within yourself to grow spiritually. You already have everything within you, and all you need to do is uncover it.

A moment of peaceful contemplation. Praying at Mount Sinai, Egypt.

CHAPTER SEVEN

WOMEN
IN ISLAM

The role of women in Islam is a complex topic. Women's rights vary widely within the Muslim world, reflecting the great variety of cultures and range of modernization and economic development among Islamic nations. In some Muslim countries, women are severely restricted in job opportunities and legal rights. On the other hand, in the early 1990s over 300 million Muslims were governed by women rulers—in Bangladesh, Pakistan, and Turkey.

THE RIGHTS OF
WOMEN

Previous page:
Muslim women praying.

An Indonesian
woman reads the
Qur'an as part
of the celebration
of a major
Islamic holiday.

It is important to remember that the behavior of individual Muslims does not always reflect the teachings of Islam. In every religion, there have been male chauvinists who have mistreated or abused women, in spite of the teachings of love and compassion found in all faiths.

Over the last hundred years, women in Western countries have gained voting and inheritance rights, as well as equal legal rights. In the poorer, less modernized countries (including many Muslim nations), women's rights have lagged behind. In other Muslim nations, especially Saudi Arabia, women still have fewer rights and freedoms than men because of a narrow-minded version of Islam, and also because of customs rooted in pre-Islamic Arab culture.

The West has stereotyped Islam as anti-women. In fact, the opposite is true. As a religion, Islam is strongly pro equality. In the seventh century, Islam gave women rights and freedoms they have only recently gained in the West. Unfortunately, Muslim societies do not always live up to the Islamic ideal.

Traditional Islamic law contains hundreds of provisions related to women's rights including:
- A woman's property is her own and cannot be seized by her husband.
- Women cannot be denied the right to education.
- Ruining a woman's reputation is a punishable offense.
- A woman cannot be forced into marriage.
- Women can file legal suits and testify in court.
- Women can freely enter into contracts.
- Spousal abuse is a punishable offense.
- Women can divorce their husbands.
- Alimony is mandatory.
- Women receive equal pay for equal work.
- Women can vote and hold office.

Both men and women are expected to follow an Islamic dress code, which basically means to dress modestly. Islamic men's dress includes the following provisions:
- Men (like women) should not wear tight clothing.
- Men who can must grow a beard.
- A turban or brimless hat is strongly recommended.
- A man must cover his body from his knees to his navel in public, at all times.

AISHAH

Beloved Wife of the Prophet ﷺ

The life of *Aishah* is a wonderful illustration that a Muslim woman can be a scholar and a teacher. *Aishah* exerted a powerful influence in the early Islamic community and provided many others with inspiration and leadership. Her talks are still read in literature courses, her legal pronouncements are studied in law schools, and her life and works have been examined by students of Muslim history for nearly 1,400 years.

In her early childhood *Aishah* was brought up by her father, *Abu Bakr*, a man of wide knowledge and the closest friend of the Prophet ﷺ. In her youth, *Aishah* was known for her striking beauty and her extraordinary memory.

Aishah married the Prophet ﷺ in 624 C.E., during the second year after the migration to Madinah, when she was about 14 or 15 years old. This was considered a normal age for marriage at that time. Before and after her wedding, *Aishah* maintained a natural gaiety and innocence. She was not overawed by her marriage to the Messenger of God, whom all his companions, including her own mother and father, treated with a level of love and reverence they gave to no one else. As his wife and close companion, she acquired from the Prophet ﷺ great depths of knowledge and insight.

Aishah was generous and patient. All the Prophet's household suffered poverty and hunger for long periods. For many days, no cooking fire would be lit in their sparsely furnished house, and they would live on dates and water. Poverty did not cause *Aishah* distress or humiliation, and when wealth did come, it did not affect her simple lifestyle. She would habitually give to the poor whatever she had and never leave anything for the next day.

During his final illness, the Prophet ﷺ went to *Aishah's* apartment. He lay there on a couch with his head resting on her breast or on her lap. Gradually his head grew heavier upon her breast, as he quietly passed away. He was buried in the floor of *Aishah's* room near the couch where he had been lying during his illness.

Aishah lived for almost 50 years after the passing away of the Prophet ﷺ. She had been his wife for nearly a decade. Much of this time was spent in learning and acquiring knowledge of the Qur'an and the hadith. *Aishah* became a *hafiz*, one who memorized the entire Qur'an. She was one of four persons who transmitted more than two thousand hadith. Many of these pertain to some of the most intimate aspects of the Prophet's ﷺ life, which only someone in *Aishah's* position could have witnessed.

Aishah was knowledgeable in law, mathematics, medicine, and poetry. Scholars regard her as one of the earliest legal experts of Islam along with the caliphs Umar and Ali. The Prophet ﷺ, referring to her extensive knowledge of Islam, is reported to have said: "Learn a portion of your religion from this lady."

Aishah also took an active part in education and social reform. She trained many boys and girls, and her house became an Islamic academy. As a teacher, she had a clear and persuasive manner of speech. One of the early Muslims said, "I have heard speeches of Abu Bakr and Umar, Uthman and Ali up to this day, but I have not heard speech more persuasive and more beautiful from the mouth of any person than from the mouth of Aishah."

Aishah was the most respected woman of her time. Men and women came from far and wide to benefit from her great knowledge. She died in the year 680 C.E. and was buried beside other companions of the Prophet ﷺ.

THE QUR'AN
AND WOMEN

The Prophet ﷺ said, "Women are the twin halves of men." That is, neither is complete without the other. The Qur'an teaches:

For Muslim men and women, for believing men and women,
for devout men and women, for true men and women,
for men and women who are patient, for men and women
        who humble themselves,
for men and women who give in charity, for men and
        women who fast,
for men and women who guard their chastity,
        and for men and women who engage much in
        God's praise—
For them all has Allah prepared forgiveness and
        great reward. (33:35)

The believers, men and women, are protectors, one
        of another:
they enjoin what is just, and forbid what is evil,
they observe regular prayers, practice regular charity,
and obey God and God's Messenger.
On them will God pour Mercy:
for God is Exalted in power, Wise. (9:71)

And their Lord answered them:
Truly I will never cause to be lost the work of any of you,
Be you a male or female, you are members one of
        another. (3:195)

Whoever works evil will not be requited but by the
        like thereof,
and whoever works a righteous deed—whether man
        or woman—
and is a believer—such will enter Paradise. (40:40)

As we can see, the Qur'an views women as spiritually equal to men. Both are God's creatures whose purpose here on earth is to worship God, do righteous deeds, and avoid evil; both will be assessed according to their actions and intentions. According to the Qur'an, a woman is required to do good deeds, the same as a man. The Qur'an has instructed all believers, women as well as men, to follow the example of ideal women from the People of the Book, such as the Virgin Mary.

One full surah (surah 58) of the Qur'an is entitled *Almujadilah* or "The woman who is arguing"; it was named after an incident involving a woman whose husband rejected her in a moment of anger. She complained to the Prophet ﷺ about her situation, and, although the Prophet ﷺ initially disagreed with her, God accepted her petition.

God has heard and accepted the statement of the woman
        who pleads with you
concerning her husband and carries her complaint to God,
and God hears the arguments between both of you
for God hears and sees all things. (58:1)

This illustrates that a woman in Islam has the right to argue even with the Prophet ﷺ himself. No one had the right to tell her to be silent, and she was under no obligation to consider her husband the final authority in matters of religion.

FATIMAH: DAUGHTER OF THE PROPHET ﷺ

Fatimah was born in Makkah. She was brought up primarily by her father, and under his guidance and inspiration, she developed into a cultured, enlightened woman. Aishah once said, "I have never come across a greater personality than that of Fatimah except that of her father, the Prophet of Islam."

Three of the Prophet's ﷺ closest companions sought her hand in marriage— Abu Bakr, Umar, and Ali. The Prophet ﷺ accepted Ali's proposal; Fatimah was 18 years old when they were married. Ali was relatively poor, and he and Fatimah worked long, hard hours to earn their livelihood. They were extremely generous and never turned away the poor. At times they gave all their food to a beggar and went hungry themselves. Fatimah became known in Madinah for her charity. On one occasion, she had nothing to eat for three days and then sold the clothes she had been wearing in order to feed a guest.

Fatimah and Ali were blessed with five children, three boys and two girls. Two of their sons, Hasan and Hussain, were the favorites of the Prophet ﷺ, who often carried them on his shoulders and let them climb on his back while he was praying.

When the Prophet ﷺ was on his deathbed, Fatimah stayed by his side. He whispered something that made her weep and then whispered something that made her smile. Later, she related that her father told her he was about to die and it made her weep, but then he told her that she would be the first person to join him in the next world and it made her smile with happiness. Fatimah passed away at the age of 28, six months after her father's death.

WOMEN AND
MARRIAGE

The Prophet ﷺ said, "The best of men is he who is best to his wife, and the best of women is she who is best to her husband." With all his responsibilities as a spiritual leader and the head of the Muslim community, Muhammad ﷺ made his own bed, sewed his own clothing, and actively participated in the chores of his household. Using a beautiful image, the Prophet ﷺ also said, "They (your wives) are your garment, and you are a garment to them." That is, men and women complete and support each other in their marriage.

The social responsibility that comes with marriage is an essential element in Islam. The Prophet taught, "Marriage is half of religion."

Under Islam, a woman retains her property when she marries. At her wedding, the bride and her family are under no obligation whatsoever to present a gift to the groom. In Islam, it is the groom who must present the bride with a marriage gift. This gift is considered her property, and neither the groom nor the bride's family have any share in or control over it. The bride retains her marriage gifts even if she is later divorced. The husband is not allowed any share in his wife's property except what she offers him with her free consent. The Qur'an states this clearly:

And give the women (on marriage) their dower as a free gift;

A muslim couple, wearing traditional dress, getting married in Karachi, Pakistan.

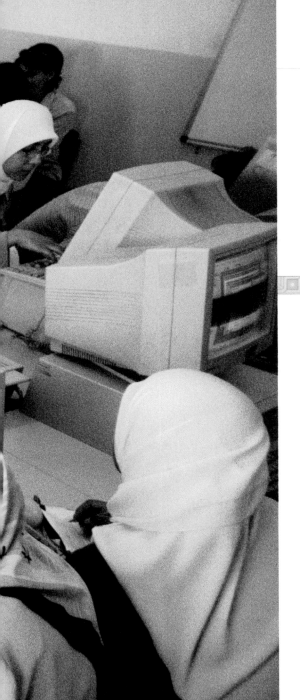

CHAPTER EIGHT

ISLAM
TODAY

Film, television, and the Internet have all contributed to deeper Islamic understanding of the West and of modern society and technology. Most modern Muslims seek to adopt and enjoy the best of Western culture, science, and technology without also rejecting their religious heritage by embracing the materialism and secular modernism that have generally accompanied these advances in the West.

ISLAM AND WESTERN
COLONIALISM

Previous page: Muslim women learning to use computers, Amman, Jordan.

Kocatepe Mosque, Ankara, Turkey, reflected in the windows of a modern office building.

In the eighteenth century, as a result of industrialization and the growth of technology, the major Western nations began to enjoy heightened economic growth as well as military power. European expansion was motivated by the desire for new markets for mass-produced goods and the need for sources of cheap raw materials; it was made possible by new technological advances in shipbuilding and weapons production.

By the beginning of the nineteenth century, the great Islamic empires had become severely weakened, and Western colonialism spread throughout the world. Europe and America held 85 percent of the Earth's surface, including most Muslim lands, in some sort of colonial subjugation.

- **1765** The powerless Mughal emperor gives control of Bengal to the British.
- **1798** Napoleon's forces invade Egypt.
- **1801** A British military expedition to Egypt defeats the French.
- **1818** Britain becomes the major power in India.
- **1864** Russia occupies all of Central Asia.
- **1914** All North Africa under European control.

By the beginning of the twentieth century, the only non-colonial Muslim states were Turkey, Iran, Saudi Arabia, and Afghanistan. From 1946, Muslim nations began to regain independence.

- **1946** France grants independence to Syria and Lebanon.
- **1947** Pakistan becomes a new nation.
- **1950** Indonesia becomes independent, after five years of revolt against the Dutch.
- **1952** Gamal Abdel Nasser deposes British puppet King Farouk.
- **1956** King Hussain of Jordan dismisses Glubb Pasha, the British officer who has commanded his army for many years.
- **1956** Morocco and Tunisia become independent from the French.
- **1958** An army coup deposes the British-supported Hashemite rulers in Iraq.

ADVICE OF ALI

Knowledge is better than wealth. Knowledge protects you, while you protect wealth. Wealth is diminished by spending, while knowledge grows by use.

Knowledge is a religion to which one is indebted; by it humanity acquires strength in life, and beauty in speech when it has been fulfilled. Knowledge is the ruler, while wealth is the ruled.

Those who accumulate wealth have perished even though they are alive, while those with knowledge last as long as time; their individualities may be gone, but their example exists in hearts. Here (pointing to his heart) I have abundant knowledge, if only I could find people to bear it. [2]

1962 Algeria gains independence from France, after years of revolt and hundreds of thousands of Algerians killed.

WESTERNIZATION

In the seventeenth and eighteenth centuries, traditional Muslim schools generally opposed the study of science and technology. From the eighth to the sixteenth century, Muslim civilizations had produced many of the world's greatest scientists and mathematicians but, as those civilizations began to break down, Islamic education became rigid and conservative.

The European colonial powers introduced Western education to their Muslim colonies. Students were taught European history and thought, from the Greeks onward. The best and brightest young Muslim students were sent to British or French universities, where they were further pressed into a European mold. The West assumed that the normal and rational response of the Muslim world was to embrace a Western, secular, materialist vision of progress.

The Western school curricula generally ignored the rich Islamic cultural heritage. Even worse, the positivist and materialistic assumptions of Western science were taught as gospel truths. Religion in general and Islam in particular were treated as outmoded, backward superstitions. As a result, the new highly educated, Westernized Muslim elite often rejected outright their Islamic heritage, or, deeply ambivalent about their religion and cultural heritage, they became self-hating Muslims.

This system created a class of highly capable, Western-educated Muslims who were alienated from their own religious and cultural roots. They often became local administrators who reported directly to their European superiors and helped form the backbone of the colonial states. The colonial nations claimed that they were training their colonies and protectorates for self-government. However, England and France set up governments ruled by puppet leaders, appointed to maintain Western political and economic interests.

"THE MOST IGNORANT AMONG YOU IS THE ONE WHO DOES NOT LEARN FROM THE CHANGES IN THE WORLD. THE RICHEST AMONG YOU IS THE ONE WHO IS NOT ENTRAPPED BY GREED." MUHAMMAD ﷺ [1]

ISLAM
IN AMERICA

Islam is an American religion. There are approximately six million Muslims in the United States. Roughly four million are Muslim immigrants and their American-born children. Two million are American converts, mainly African Americans. The first known Muslim prayer group in the United States was organized in 1900 in Ross, North Dakota. The first officially designated mosque was established in Cedar Rapids, Iowa, in 1934.

IMMIGRATION

A mosque in Washington DC, USA, combining elements of Eastern and Western architecture.

In the late nineteenth century, Muslims from what are now known as Syria, Lebanon, and Jordan began to emigrate to the United States. Most were unskilled laborers with little education. Many became factory workers or peddlers. Following World War II, a new wave of immigration began. Many of these immigrants were political refugees, fleeing communism or oppressive rule in various Middle Eastern countries. Many were well educated.

More recently, from the late 1960s on, the majority of Muslim immigrants have come seeking advanced training and professional employment. They are well-educated professionals, fluent in English.

There are also a significant number of foreign Muslim students in American universities. Estimates of the number of foreign Muslim students range from 200,000 to 800,000. They have established Muslim student organizations on over one hundred campuses and sponsor Friday prayers, Islamic holiday celebrations, Islamic conferences, and other activities. Many of these students have sought professional employment in the United States upon graduation. Others have returned home to positions of business or political leadership.

"TRUE SERVANTS OF GOD, THE MOST GRACIOUS, ARE THEY WHO WALK GENTLY ON THE EARTH, AND WHO, WHENEVER THE IGNORANT ADDRESS THEM, REPLY WITH WORDS OF PEACE." MUHAMMAD 3

Broccoli for Breakfast: An American Muslim's Ramadan

"I make phone calls to waiting friends, 'Ramadan Mubarak'—Blessings of Ramadan. It has begun! There is something [exciting] about sharing in a practice that is over 14 centuries old.

"This is not something new. The One God has delivered the One Message through the millennia and each messenger has instructed his people in the practice of fasting. '. . . for to fast is to do good unto yourself if you but knew it.' (2:184) That's where the faith comes in. For the love of Allah I make my inner intention (niyah) to fast each day; for the love of Allah I embrace hunger and thirst and loss of sleep; for the love of Allah I surrender to this obligation—praying to increase my hunger and thirst for Allah. And in this process I get to do my own inner jihad with the nafs at all stages: with pride, anger, envy, appetite, and blame. For as it says in the Tradition of the Prophet Muhammad ﷺ: 'If a person does not give up falsehood and false conduct during the fast, Allah does not need his hunger and thirst.'

"So the rhythm of Ramadan sweeps me up from comforts, tosses aside habits, and leaves me parched and empty in the lengthening shadows of the late afternoon. Feeling raw and vulnerable to confrontations and cranky responses, the breath gets slower and deeper. Remember Allah with each pang of discomfort. Remember: there are many people much more intimate with real starvation who have no hope of an evening meal. Remember: the incredible abundance we all take for granted. Remember: this emptiness is a blessing, a hollow accommodation for clarity. Remember: we are all united in Allah's Mercy.

"As the sun sinks below the horizon I prepare to break the fast with water and dates. 'Bismillah. Ya Allah, I fast for You. I trust in You and You alone and I break the

fast with Your abundant gifts.' The sweetness of the first sips of water flows into my body, which sighs gratefully. Alhamdulillah! We give thanks to Allah for all His support in helping us to complete another day of fasting.

"One thing I always notice with surprise is how easy some things are in this month. It's always easier to get up in the very early morning. I feel like there is a Presence helping, offering extra support and protection. It is almost impossible to oversleep even when the night is too short. Eating so early in the morning is totally weird for me, but this year I have discovered broccoli for breakfast! It seems to be just what my body needs. I learn a lot about intention during Ramadan—renewing it every day is essential and I'm seeing that whatever I do consistently, with intention, has a long-term effect. As a co-worker noted, 'I'm interested in how this changes you.' That to me is the yardstick. If it's not changing me—it's not real.

"Every year I get stripped down, reduced to rawness, by fasting for Allah, and nourished by extra prayers and study. I get to return to a more natural state and rhythm where intimacy with Allah is all there is. Now, as we await the sighting of the new moon, there is some sadness and apprehension, knowing that some things will be harder again. I will miss the wake-up calls, the heightened sensitivity, the sunset gatherings with friends to break the fast, pray, and eat together, the deep sharing—just by a glance from one exposed soul to another—and the protection that surrounds us. But I also feel stronger as I step back into the rhythms of the world. The drum-beat of truth is a little louder in my heart, the guardian against idle gossip and anger is more present to show another way, and I can still have broccoli for breakfast and Remember." [4]

AFRICAN-AMERICAN MUSLIMS

Some scholars have estimated that as many as one out of five slaves brought to North and South America were Muslim. In almost every case their religious and cultural roots were destroyed, and they were quickly converted to Christianity.

The first African American to turn toward Islam as a way of uniting his community was Timothy Drew, born in 1886 in North Carolina. In 1913 he changed his name to Noble Drew Ali and founded the Moorish-American Science Temple in Newark, New Jersey. He taught a mixture of Eastern philosophy which he called Islam and insisted that Christianity was for whites and Islam was the religion of the "Asiatics," including Africans. He and his followers opened temples in several cities, but his movement has remained small up until today.

In 1929, W. D. Fard began to teach another self-developed religious system that he called Islam. Fard's origins are obscure, although he claimed to have been born in Makkah to a European mother and Arab father. He insisted that all African Americans were Muslims who had lost their roots, and he called his religious movement "The Lost-Found Nation of Islam in the Wilderness of North America."

Fard was succeeded by Elijah Muhammad, who stressed certain un-Islamic ideas like the rejection of all whites, whom he called Satan. He also introduced traditional Islamic teachings, forbidding drugs, alcohol, adultery, gambling, and eating pork.

This movement became called The Nation of Islam. It provided a positive identity, successful role models, and renewed self-esteem for many hundreds of thousands of African Americans.

The Nation of Islam has been either ignored or criticized by the U.S. media. Characterized as a rabidly anti-white, sectarian cult, the Nation was never accepted by most Americans as a legitimate religious movement.

Malcolm X, the best-known spokesman for the Nation of Islam, performed the pilgrimage to Makkah and encountered an Islam of tolerance and brotherhood very different from what he had been taught. He broke with Elijah Muhammad after his return. Shortly after, Malcolm X was assassinated by members of the Nation of Islam.

When Elijah Muhammad died in 1975, his son Warith Deen Muhammad succeeded him. Warith Deen almost immediately began the process of bringing the teachings and practices of the Nation of Islam in line with traditional Islam. The Nation's temples were renamed mosques and the ministers called imams. Warith Deen formally disavowed the old anti-white and heterodox teachings of his father, and this movement has become an accepted part of Islam in America, acknowledged by Islamic leaders around the world.

A significant minority of the old Nation of Islam, led by Minister Louis Farrakhan, continued Elijah Muhammad's original teachings and also kept the organization's name. Farrakhan has continued to preach against the worldwide oppression of blacks by whites. However, he has also encouraged his followers to follow traditional Islamic practices and has sought and gained acceptance from Islamic leaders and scholars.

Unfortunately, in spite of its growing number of adherents, Islam is not yet recognized as a major American religious movement.

Reverend Farrakhan with members of the Nation of Islam speaking in New York in 1985.

A Letter from Makkah by Malcolm X

Never have I witnessed such overwhelming spirit of hospitality and true brotherhood as is practiced by people *of all colors* and races here in this Ancient Holy Land, the home of Abraham, Muhammad, and all the other Prophets of the Holy Scriptures. For the past week, I have been utterly speechless and spellbound by the graciousness I see displayed all around me by people of all colors. . . .

There were tens of thousands of pilgrims, from all over the world. They were of all colors, from blue-eyed blonds to black-skinned Africans. But we were all participating in the same ritual displaying a spirit of unity and brotherhood that my experiences in America had led me to believe never could exist between the white and the nonwhite.

America needs to understand Islam, because this is the one religion that erases from its society the race problem. Throughout my travels in the Muslim world, I have met, talked to, and even eaten with people who in America would have been considered "white"—but the "white" attitude was removed from their minds by the religion of Islam. I have never before seen *sincere* and *true* brotherhood practiced by all colors together, irrespective of their color.

You may be shocked by these words coming from me. But on this pilgrimage, what I have seen, and experienced, has forced me to *rearrange* much of my thought-patterns previously held, and to *toss aside* some of my previous conclusions. . . .

During the past eleven days here in the Muslim world, I have eaten from the same

plate, drunk from the same glass, and slept in the same bed (or on the same rug)—while praying to the *same God*—with fellow Muslims, whose eyes were the bluest of blue, whose hair was the blondest of blond, and whose skin was the whitest of white. And in the *words* and in the *actions* and in the *deeds* of the "white" Muslims, I felt the same sincerity that I felt among the black African Muslims of Nigeria, Sudan, and Ghana.

We were truly all the same (brothers)—because their belief in one God had removed the "white" from their *minds*, the "white" from their behavior, and the "white" from their *attitude*. I could see from this, that perhaps if white Americans could accept the Oneness of God, then perhaps, too, they could accept in reality the Oneness of Man—and cease to measure, and hinder, and harm others in terms of the "differences" in color. . . .

All praise is due to Allah, the Lord of all the Worlds,

Sincerely,
El-Hajj Malik El-Shabazz
(Malcolm X)

Malcom X speaks to a crowd in Harlem at a rally in support of integration measures in Birmingham, Alabama.

ISLAM IN BRITAIN
AND EUROPE

In 1641 British records mention for the first time Muslims living in London. The first English version of the Qur'an was published in 1649. However, the current British Muslim population is comparatively recent, based primarily on the immigration of Muslims from the Indian subcontinent since the 1950s.

After World War II, Britain, Germany, and France had serious manpower shortages and encouraged immigration from former colonies and other developing countries. There are from 1.5 million to 2 million Muslims in Britain today, mainly in the large metropolitan centers of London, Birmingham, Manchester, and Glasgow. Over two thirds are British-born with roots in Pakistan, India, and Bangladesh. There are also sizeable communities from Africa, Turkey, and the Middle East, together with more recent refugees from Afghanistan, Iran, Iraq, Bosnia, Somalia, and Albania. Islam is now the second largest religion in Britain. There are over four thousand British Islamic organizations. Some are political, and others are educational, religious, or charitable.

In France, estimates of the Muslim population range from four to five million. Most French Muslims have their roots in North Africa. The first influx came in the early twentieth century and was composed mainly of unskilled workers. More immigrants came during the world wars and then immediately after World War II, when there was a major labor shortage in France.

There are 3.5 million Muslims in Germany. The majority are Turkish or of Turkish descent. Following World War II, Germany invited in large numbers of Turkish "guest workers" as a temporary labor pool, and many stayed. There are also significant German Muslim communities who came from the Balkans and also from North Africa.

According to the Central Institute Islamic Archives in Soest, Germany, there are approximately 33.4 million Muslims in Europe today, and the Muslim population is growing rapidly at 6.5 percent a year. There are 25 million Muslims in Russia, including Chechnya and Siberia. There are 5.7 million Muslims living in European Turkey. In the Balkans there are approximately 2 million Muslims in Bosnia, 2 million in Kosovo, and 1.5 million in Bulgaria.

The golden dome and minaret of a mosque built in London, in the 1980s.

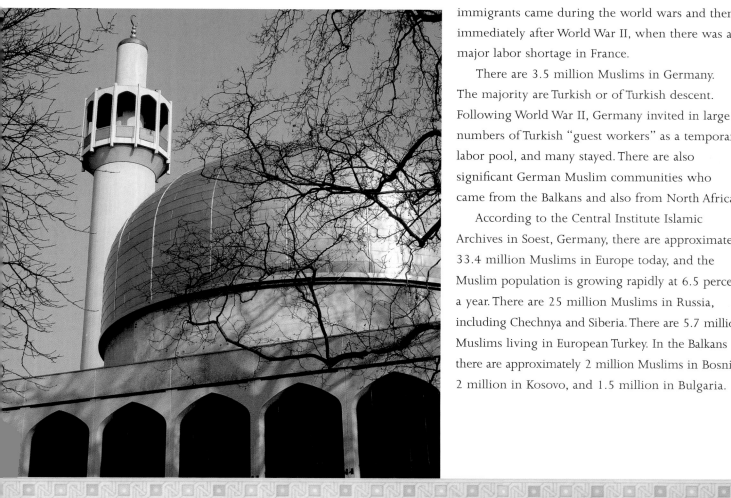

ISLAM AND THE
MODERN WORLD

Third-world activists opposed to the excesses of colonialism and capitalism used to be called communists. Today Muslim activists are labeled "Islamic fundamentalists." In most Muslim countries, intelligent people have resisted Western capitalist exploitation, which has included stripping natural resources and raw materials for extremely low prices, mistreatment and underpayment of workers, and encouragement of consumerism and desire for Western mass-produced goods.

The label of "fundamentalism" generally does not fit Islam. It was originally used for an early twentieth-century Christian revivalist movement that believed in taking as literally true the words of the King James Bible. A better word for the Islamic response to the Western, materialist model of progress would be "Islamism."

The first major Islamist movement was the Muslim Brotherhood, founded in 1928 in Egypt and centered at Al-Azhar University in Cairo. The Brotherhood advocated a progressive view of the Shariah, one that emphasized individual reasoning and discovery. Muslims have continued to look for alternatives to Western secular materialism and have sought ways to combine Islam with the challenges of modern society.

The Muslim Brotherhood sought to develop a new, Islamic model of modernization. It stressed the importance of modern education combined with Islamic values, and dismissed as out of touch with reality the orthodox *ulama* who rejected all Western ideas as "un-Islamic." The Brotherhood has been a major political influence in Egypt, Syria, Yemen, and the Sudan.

The Iranian revolution provided an inspirational example to Islamist movements around the world. In spite of its extreme elements, Muslims saw, for the first time, a modern Islamic state that proudly maintained economic and political independence from the West.

It is only natural that intelligent Muslims are seeking new alternatives. The basic features of the new Islamic movements include a belief that Islam is a comprehensive way of life that includes society, politics, and economics. There is also an understanding that Western secularism and materialism are incompatible with Islam.

Many Muslims feel that the renewal of their society requires a return to Islam as a response to the Western education and secular values imposed on the last few generations by the colonial powers. This includes replacing present Western-derived legal systems with laws based on Islam. Science and technology are to be accepted but studied and applied within a framework of Islamic values. Change also requires social and political struggle against corruption and social injustice.

"KNOWLEDGE THAT IS NOT BENEFICIAL

IS LIKE A TREASURE THAT YOU CANNOT

SPEND." MUHAMMAD ﷺ 5

AL-KHWARIZMI, THE GREATEST MATHEMATICIAN

Muhammad al-Khwarizmi (780–847 C.E.) was born in what is today Uzbekistan and lived in Baghdad. He was one of the greatest mathematicians and scientists of all time. He is the founder of algebra, whose name is derived from his famous book on elementary mathematics, *Kitab al-jabr wa al-muqabah.* This book was translated into Latin and used until the sixteenth century as the principal mathematical textbook in European universities. Al-Khwarizmi was also the founder of several other branches of mathematics. He is best known for introducing the mathematical concept algorithm, which is named after him.

Al-Khwarizmi had a greater influence on mathematical thought than any other medieval writer. He was the first systematizer of algebra; he provided analytical solutions of linear and quadratic equations. He adopted the use of zero, leading to the arithmetic of positions and the decimal system. In addition to introducing the Arabic numerals, he developed several basic arithmetical procedures, including operations on fractions. He developed trigonometric tables containing the sine functions, and refined the geometric representation of conic sections.

Al-Khwarizmi was also a great astronomer and geographer. In addition to an important treatise on astronomy, he wrote a book on astronomical tables, which was translated into several European languages and even into Chinese. His contribution to geography is also outstanding. He revised Greek geographical theories and devised new and improved measurement techniques. Seventy geographers worked under al-Khwarizmi's leadership and, in 830 C.E., they produced the first map of the globe. In addition to his scientific work, Al-Khwarizmi also wrote influential books on music and history.

A famous ayah from the Qur'an.

MODERN ISLAMIC MOVEMENTS

Modern Islamic movements share the following basic premises:

- God is the ultimate authority over humanity. This means any government must be limited by certain basic moral and ethical principles, including ecology, care for the welfare of all people (as well as animals, plants, water, and air), and government as a service both to the people and to our highest ideals.

- Equality of all people. Islam teaches that we are all one family, descended from Adam and Eve. The Qur'an clearly teaches equality.

Behold,
We have created you all out of a male and a female,
and have made you into nations and tribes, so that you
might come to know one another. Verily, the noblest of
you in the sight of God is the one who is most
pious. (49:13)

THE CASE OF IRAN

The best-known Islamist movement has been the movement that created the Iranian revolution of 1978–1979 C.E., which replaced the strongly Western and modernist shah with the government headed by the Ayatollah Khomeini.

Reza Shah and his son ruled Iran for over 50 years, from 1925 until 1979 C.E.. Reza Shah was determined to modernize Iran. He considered the Iranian religious establishment an obstacle to progress and confiscated the funds and properties held in trust for the mosques and other religious institutions. Religious leaders who criticized the shah or his policies were jailed or tortured.

Reza Shah was strongly pro-German, and in 1941 C.E., Soviet and British forces invaded Iran in order to prevent the shah from supporting the Nazi government. The British arrested him, forced him to abdicate, and sent him into exile on a British warship. He was succeeded by his 21-year-old son, Muhammad Reza. Shah Muhammad Reza's rule was heavily supported by British and American oil interests. He received huge amounts of U.S. aid in return for his support of American Middle East policies. His secret police force, Savak, was feared throughout Iran, and it ruthlessly suppressed any opposition to the shah or his modernization policies.

In spite of government repression, opposition to the shah steadily grew. Many felt that Muhammad Reza's rush to Westernization was causing Iran to lose its identity and become a poor copy of Western nations.

A public uprising, inspired primarily by the Iranian cleric Khomeini, overthrew the shah in 1979 C.E.. Khomeini and his supporters set up the government for the world's first modern Islamic republic. Just as the shah forced Westernization on the Iranian people, Khomeini enforced

Islamicization. His interpretation of Islam became law, and like the shah, he ruthlessly suppressed any opposition. Until Khomeini's death in 1989 C.E., opposition meant jail or even death.

Khomeini's extremist position gained the attention of the world. He insisted that the purpose of government was to administer the Shariah and that only the religious authorities were qualified to handle the affairs of the government. He actively opposed Western values and criticized the United States in particular.

During Khomeini's ten-year rule, Iran suffered eight years of war with Iraq as well as bloody internal strife with Iranian Kurds and Communists. The Soviets supported the Iranian Communists, and the Iraqis and the Kurds were heavily supported by the West. This was a result of Iran's opposition to the West, but it was also due to fears that a movement for independent Islamic self-rule might spread and overthrow other pro-Western or Communist puppet governments.

Ayatollah Khomeini, chief of the religious opposition to the shah of Iran, in exile, at Neuphle Le Chateau, France.

THE WAHABI MOVEMENT

Another major Islamic movement is the Wahabi movement. Muhammad al-Wahab (1703–1787) was an Arab theologian who lived in the homeland of the Saudi tribe. In 1744 he began a campaign to purify and renew Islam in Arabia. Wahab sought to return to what he believed was the authentic Islam of the Prophet ﷺ and to remove all later additions and customs. He preached an inflexible approach to Islam that has included insistence on the veiling and subjugation of women, harsh penalties for minor crimes, and unthinking rejection of most modern values. If the label of fundamentalism fits any aspect of Islam, it fits the Wahabi position.

When the Saudis took control of Arabia, they brought Wahab's doctrines with them. Using their immense wealth and influence, the Saudis have spread the Wahabi movement beyond Saudi Arabia. The Afghan Taliban, for example, was composed of refugee students who were educated in Saudi-run religious schools in Pakistan and indoctrinated in the Wahabi version of Islam. The Saudis set up over 7,500 schools in the area.

Veiled Muslim woman, Gaza Strip, Middle East, 1990s.

AZ-ZAHRAWI, THE FATHER OF MODERN SURGERY

Abul Qasim az-Zahrawi (936–1013 C.E.) was the greatest surgeon of the Middle Ages. He is best known for his major advances in surgical techniques, as an inventor of surgical instruments, and for his 30-volume medical encyclopedia, which covered every aspect of the medical knowledge of his day. The encyclopedia was translated into Latin, Hebrew, French, and English. It was an essential text in the medical curriculum in European countries for centuries.

Az-Zahrawi grew up in Córdoba, the capital of Muslim Spain, where he served as court physician. Patients and medical students from all over Europe came to him for treatment and training.

Three volumes of az-Zahrawi's encyclopedia deal with surgery, including his own inventions and procedures. The last volume includes diagrams and illustrations of more than two hundred surgical instruments, most of which az-Zahrawi developed himself. Az-Zahrawi gave detailed descriptions of many surgical operations, including the removal of bladder stones; eye, ear, and throat surgery; midwifery; and amputation. These three volumes laid the foundation for Western surgery.

Az-Zahrawi also discussed the preparation of medicines and prescribed the use of diuretics, purgatives, and hot baths. He was the first to give a detailed description of hemophilia and the first to use silk thread for stitching wounds. He pioneered the use of cauterization and listed fifty diseases to be treated with cauterization techniques. Az-Zahrawi was also an expert in oral surgery and dentistry. He designed dental instruments and developed new dental procedures including realigning and extracting teeth, and the preparation and setting of artificial teeth.

ISLAM'S OPPOSITION TO VIOLENCE AND TERRORISM

Before discussing what Islam actually teaches about violence and terrorism, it is important to look at the bias and distortion generally found in the Western media when covering Islam. All too often Islam is treated as one simple set of beliefs or practices. This treatment is partly fiction, partly ideological stereotype, and minimally the religion and culture of Islam. There is no correspondence between the Islam of the media and the enormously rich and complex reality of the world of Islam, which includes over a billion people and dozens of societies and cultures with their own histories and geographies.

One critic of the popular analyses of Islam has pointed out, "In many instances 'Islam' has licensed not only patent inaccuracy but also expressions of unrestrained ethnocentrism, cultural and even racial hatred, deep yet paradoxically free-floating hostility. All this has taken place as part of what is presumed to be fair, balanced, responsible coverage of Islam." [7]

Therefore, in examining the topic of Islam and terrorism, we must begin by taking with a pinch of salt much of what we have heard or read, especially the frequent connection between Islam and terrorism. Those who advocate terrorism and the killing of innocent civilians do not represent Islam. Their statements and actions directly contradict the most fundamental Islamic teachings. Just as Hitler and Nazism represent serious distortions of the Christian civilization and culture from which they arose, Muslim terrorists and Islamic organizations that advocate violence have distorted the basic teachings and values of Islam.

Islamic law opposes all uses of violence except in the case of war or the legally sanctioned punishment of criminals. Even in war, the inflicting of any injury to women and children is forbidden

and so is the use of force against civilians. Enemy soldiers on the battlefield must be met with force, and it is only in battle that injurious physical force can be used. Violence outside of this context is forbidden by Islamic law. This includes the prohibition of harming even a single plant or tree owned by the enemy.

Kuwaiti Muslim woman holding a candle.

The Qur'an clearly teaches:

> Fight in God's cause against those who wage war on you,
> but do not commit aggression—
> For truly, God does not love aggressors. (2:190)

"GOD WILL NOT HAVE MERCY UPON A PERSON WHO HAS NO MERCY UPON OTHERS." MUHAMMAD ﷺ [8]

ALI AND THE INNER *JIHAD*

Ali was one of the finest and most fearless Muslim warriors. He was known as the lion of Islam. During the battle of Badr, Ali knocked the sword out of the hand of an enemy fighter and raised his sword to finish the man off. The enemy spit in Ali's face. Ali stepped back, sheathed his sword and exclaimed, "Go, it is now unlawful for me to take your life!" The man said, "I don't understand. You were just about to kill me, and when I spit in your face, I saw you get angry. So why did you refuse to kill me as you had planned?"

Ali answered, "Because I became angry I cannot slay you. I will fight and even kill for the sake of God, but I will not become a murderer for the sake of my ego."

A fundamental principle in the Qur'an is that the only justification for war is self-defense. Islam stands totally opposed to the use of unjust, violent force against the rights and persons of others. This includes not only Muslims but also followers of Judaism and Christianity, who are considered People of the Book. The Prophet ﷺ taught, "By God, they are not true Muslims from whose mischief their neighbor does not feel secure."

The Prophet ﷺ also stressed that caring for others is an essential element of Islam. He said, "There is a piece of flesh which, if healthy, the whole body is healthy, and which, if diseased, the whole body is diseased. This piece of flesh is the heart." Certainly hatred and violence will lead to the disease of the heart. Whenever we close our hearts to others we close our hearts to God.

Some Muslim leaders have used the term jihad as "holy war," in the sense of a war against the West as an enemy of Islam. This term has been embraced by the Western media when writing about Islam. However, as mentioned earlier in this book, jihad literally means "struggle" and is generally used in the sense of inner struggle to follow the path of God. In fact, there is no word in Arabic for "holy war." The term was coined in Europe for the Crusades, the war initiated by Christians against Muslims.

The violence that does exist in Islamic society is due not to the teachings of Islam, but to the failings of the human followers of Islam. No religion can overcome completely our human imperfection, and all religions have been misused to justify violence and oppression.

Sheikh Muhaiyadeen, a Sufi master from Sri Lanka who lived and taught in the United States, exhorted all Americans to follow the highest principles of unity and compassion found in Islam.

"JIHAD IS NOT TAKING A SWORD AND FIGHTING ON THE WAY OF GOD. JIHAD IS TAKING CARE OF YOUR PARENTS AND CHILDREN AND BEING FREE FROM NEEDING OTHERS." MUHAMMAD ﷺ [9]

"The light of Islam should reveal the essence of God in every life. If we see that essence, then we will live in unity; we will eat from the same plate; we will live as one family whether some are in a church, some are in a mosque, or some are in their homes. The beggar and the king will be able to pray together. We will discover our own faults, discard our own anger, and embrace one another with love. That is what the Qur'an says. That is why we cannot tell lies, indulge in treachery, or threaten to kill other lives and claim that it is being done in the name of Islam. Islam teaches that we must recognize and praise the essence of God as it exists in each and every life." [11]

THE PROMISE OF ISLAM

Our Western developments of modernization and technology have brought about a revolution in information systems, great medical advances, and major scientific breakthroughs. However, these developments have also been accompanied by increasing pollution, the depletion of natural resources, an ever-increasing gap between the haves and the have-nots, and other serious world problems. Perhaps some of the answers to developing a healthier, ecological, and human-centered approach to growth can be found in Islam. Instead of opposing Islam in the West, we can come to greater mutual understanding and to a greater recognition of the importance of Islamic values and traditions for all of the modern world, East and West alike.

"PROTECT AND HONOR THE EARTH, FOR THE EARTH IS YOUR MOTHER." MUHAMMAD ﷺ 10

Minarets and rooftops in Istanbul, Turkey.

Mosques silhouetted against the sun setting over Cairo, Egypt.

In a speech given on September 26, 2001, while the United States was still reeling from the attacks on the World Trade Center and the Pentagon, Carly Fiorina, the Chief Executive Officer of the Hewlett-Packard Corporation and the senior woman business executive in the United States, gave a speech that is excerpted here:

In Praise of Islamic Civilization

There was once a civilization that was the greatest in the world. It was able to create a continental super-state that stretched from ocean to ocean, and from northern climes to tropics and deserts. Within its dominion lived hundreds of millions of people, of different creeds and ethnic origins.

One of its languages became the universal language of much of the world, the bridge between the peoples of a hundred lands. Its armies were made up of people of many nationalities, and its military protection allowed a degree of peace and prosperity that had never been known. The reach of this civilization's commerce extended from Latin America to China, and everywhere in between.

And this civilization was driven more than anything by invention. Its architects designed buildings that defied gravity. Its mathematicians created the algebra and algorithms that would enable the building of computers, and the creation of encryption. Its doctors examined the human body, and found new cures for disease. Its astronomers looked into the heavens, named the stars, and paved the way for space travel and exploration.

Its writers created thousands of stories . . . of courage, romance and magic. Its poets wrote of love, when others before them were too steeped in fear to think of such things.

When other nations were afraid of ideas, this civilization thrived on them, and kept them alive. When censors threatened to wipe out knowledge from past civilizations, this civilization kept the knowledge alive, and passed it on to others.

While modern Western civilization shares many of these traits, the civilization I'm talking about was the Islamic world from the year 800 to 1600, which included the Ottoman empire and the courts of Baghdad, Damascus, and Cairo, and enlightened rulers like Suleiman the Magnificent.

Although we are often unaware of our indebtedness to this other civilization, its gifts are very much a part of our heritage. The technology industry would not exist without the contributions of Arab mathematicians. Sufi poet-philosophers like Rumi challenged our notions of self and truth. Leaders like Suleiman contributed to our notions of tolerance and civic leadership.

And perhaps we can learn a lesson from his example: it was leadership based on meritocracy, not inheritance. It was leadership that harnessed the full capabilities of a very diverse population that included Christianity, Islamic, and Jewish traditions.

This kind of enlightened leadership—leadership that nurtured culture, sustainability, diversity, and courage—led to 800 years of invention and prosperity. In dark and serious times like this, we must affirm our commitment to building societies and institutions that aspire to this kind of greatness. [12]

EXPERIENCE ISLAM

ALL THINGS COME FROM GOD

Muslims believe that all things come to us from God. God works through others to provide us with our sustenance, with help and support, and with caring and love.

For one day, count all the blessings and gifts you receive. Look for the hidden hand of God behind everything you receive, and then thank God for all you have been given.

SEEK KNOWLEDGE DAILY

In a famous *hadith*, the Prophet ﷺ taught, "If one day you are the same as the day before, that day is a loss." In other words, seek to grow and to learn more every day. For a week, write in your daily journal what you learned each day. Your new learning should not be simply reading a newspaper or listening to the nightly news report. Learn something new each day, something that you can put into practice. It can be as simple as learning how to cook a soft-boiled egg or how to hammer a nail properly.

RETREAT

Retreat has been a part of every religious tradition. All the great prophets had their times of retreat from the distractions of the world. One example is Moses meeting God in the midst of the desert, and later going up Mount Sinai to receive the teachings of the Torah. Muhammad ﷺ was on retreat in a cave on Mount Hira when the first lines of the Qur'an were revealed to him. The desert fathers of early Christianity made retreat their major spiritual practice. Native Americans practiced the vision quest.

You can carry out a retreat at home, at the house of a vacationing friend, or in a hotel room. Unplug the telephone and the TV. Remove from sight books, magazines, and other distractions. Close the curtains or cover the windows so you cannot see out or be seen.

Begin the retreat by formally making intention that you will dedicate this time for your own spiritual nourishment, that you will remain in silence and solitude for the entire retreat period. You can try a retreat for 24 hours or less, but three or four days is preferable.

Take a shower each morning, praying to God to help you cleanse yourself within and without. Eat lightly or fast from dawn to sundown. Do not let your meals take up too much time and energy.

During your retreat you can pray, sit still and contemplate your life, or meditate on some aspect of the divine. You can also read scripture or the writings of a great saint, but do not let reading fill all your time. Read for ten or fifteen minutes and then contemplate what you have read for at least half an hour or more.

The essential core of the retreat is to become more and more quiet and still inside. Slow down and let your mind focus on God instead of being distracted by all the business and busyness of the world. It may take some time to get used to remaining in silence; however, the retreat should be a pleasure and not an ordeal. Look on the retreat as a time to nourish your soul.

AUTHOR'S NOTES

Introduction

1 It is customary in Islam to refer to the great prophets with the designation "peace be upon them" and the Prophet Muhammad with "peace and blessings upon him." I have shown this in the text as ﷺ and ﷺ.

2 Angha, Nahid. 1995. *Deliverance: Words from the Prophet Mohammad*. San Rafael, CA: International Association of Sufism. p. 90.

Chapter One

1 *Ibid*. p. 66.

2 Wolfe, Michael. 1993. *The Hadj*. New York: Grove Press. pp. 16–17.

3 Fadiman, James, and Frager, Robert. 1997. *Essential Sufism*. San Francisco: HarperSanFrancisco. p. 189.

4 Hoffman, Murad. 2001. *Journey to Islam*: Leicester, UK: The Islamic Foundation. pp. 72–73, 201–202.

5 An unpublished interview with Meryam Pomeroy, conducted by Hilel Sala.

Chapter Two

1 C.E. means "Common Era," referring to the Western calendar. The Islamic calendar dates year one to the first year of *hijra*, the journey made by the Muslim community from Makkah to Madinah. For the sake of simplicity I have used only the Western calendar in this book.

2 Cleary, Thomas. 2001. *The Wisdom of the Prophet*. Boston: Shambhala. p. 46.

3 Author's translation.

4 Hoffman, Murad. 2001. *Journey to Islam*. Leicester, UK: The Islamic Foundation. pp. 95–96.

Chapter Three

1 Ozak, Muzaffer. 1999. *Love is the Wine*, 2nd Edition (Robert Frager, Ed.). Los Angeles: Philosophical Research Press. p. 35.

2 Angha, Nahid. 1995. *Deliverance: Words from the Prophet Mohammad*. San Rafael, CA: International Association of Sufism, p. 39.

3 Bucaille, Maurice. 1978. *The Bible, the Qur'an and Science*. Indianapolis, IN: American Trust Publications. p. 120.

4 Author's translation.

5 Ibn al-Qayyim in Roger Du Pasquier. 1992. *Unveiling Islam*. Cambridge, UK: Islamic Texts Society. pp. 29–30.

Chapter Four

1 Du Pasquier, Roger. 1992. *Unveiling Islam*. Cambridge, UK: Islamic Texts Society. p. 45.

2 Mohammed, J. (Ed.). 2000. *Gems of Wisdom, Heart of Gold*. Milpitas, CA: Pyramid Connections. p. 73.

3 *Ibid*. p. 56.

4 Angha, Nahid. 1995, *Deliverance: Words from the Prophet Mohammad*. San Rafael, CA: International Association of Sufism. p. 39.

5 *Ibid*. p. 19.

6 *Ibid*. p. 76.

7 *Ibid*. p. 37.

8 *Ibid*. p. 37.

9 *Ibid*. p. 71.

10 *Ibid*. p. 41.

11 Robinson, Francis (Ed.). 1996. *The Cambridge Illustrated History of the Islamic World*. Cambridge, U.K.: Cambridge University Press. p. 78.

12 Dale, Stephen. 1996. "The Islamic World in the Age of European Expansion 1500–1800. In Robinson, Francis (Ed.). *The Cambridge Illustrated History of the Islamic World*. Cambridge, UK: University of Cambridge Press. p. 78.

13 Fadiman, James and Frager, Robert. 1997. *Essential Sufism*. San Francisco: HarperSanFrancisco. p. 81.

Chapter Five

1 Although Islamic education traditionally included Sufism along with the study of philosophy and theology, there are large numbers of Muslims today, especially from Arab countries, who have never been exposed to Sufism, and who believe it is not truly part of Islam. This is in great part because their rationalist approach to religion neither understands nor accepts mysticism.

2 Fadiman, James and Frager, Robert. 1997. *Essential Sufism*. San Francisco: HarperSanFrancisco. p. 36.

3 Frager, Robert. 1999. *Heart, Self, and Soul*. Wheaton, IL: Quest Books. p. 187.

4 Fadiman and Frager, *op. cit*. p. 15.

5 Author's translation.

6 Ladinsky, D. 1996. *I Heard God Laughing: Renderings of Hafiz*. Walnut Creek, CA: Sufism Reoriented, p. 109.

7 Nurbakhsh, Javad. 1981. *Traditions of the Prophet*. New York: Khaniqahi-Nimatullahi Publications. p. 71.

8 Field, Reshad. 1976. *The Last Barrier*. New York: Harper & Row. pp. 68–69.

9 Angha, Nahid. 1995. *Deliverance: Words from the Prophet Mohammad*. San Rafael, CA: International Association of Sufism. p. 78.

10 Author's translation.

11 Nurbakhsh. *op. cit*. p. 69.

12 Ozelsel, Michaela. 1996. *Forty Days: The Diary of a Traditional Solitary Sufi Retreat*. Brattleboro, VT: Threshold. pp. 38, 90–91, 104–105.

13 Fadiman and Frager, *op. cit*. p. 61.

14 Mohammed, J. (Ed.). 2000. *Gems of Wisdom, Heart of Gold*. Milpitas, CA: Pyramid Connections. pp. 53–55.

15 Fadiman and Frager, *op. cit*. p. 244.

16 Author's translation.

17 Rumi. *The Essential Rumi* (Coleman Barks, Transl.). San Francisco: HarperSanFrancisco. p. 36.

18 *Ibid*

19 *Ibid*. p. 279.

20 *Ibid*. pp. 193–194.

21 *Ibid* p. 171.

22 Ladinsky, D. 1996. *I Heard God Laughing, Renderings of Hafiz*. Walnut Creek, CA: Sufism Reoriented, p. 63.

Chapter Six

1 There is no single Islamic psychology. Sufi masters and others have provided many different descriptions of human nature. In this chapter I have distilled several of the major elements common to most of these descriptions. For a more detailed analysis of Sufi psychology, see R. Frager. 1999. *Heart, Self, and Soul*. Wheaton, IL: Quest Books.

2 The terms heart (*qalb*) and soul (*ruh*) have a range of meanings in Sufi and Islamic psychologies. Although I am following well-accepted usage, the reader should be aware that these terms have other meanings as well. For example, *ruh* is sometimes used for individual soul, but it is also used for universal spirit.

3 Angha, Nahid. 1995. *Deliverance: Words from the Prophet Mohammad*. San Rafael, CA: International Association of Sufism. p. 49.

4 *Ibid*. p. 73.

5 Jilani, A. 1992. *The Secret of Secrets* (Tosun Bayrak, Transl.). Cambridge, UK: Islamic Texts Society. p. xlvii.

6 Hoffman, Murad. 2001. *Journey to Islam*. Leicester, UK: The Islamic Foundation. pp. 59–61.

7 Frager, Robert. 1999. *Heart, Self, and Soul*. Wheaton, IL: Quest. p. 23.

8 Fadiman, James and Frager, Robert. 1997. *Essential Sufism*. San Francisco: HarperSanFrancisco. p. 232.

9 Rumi. 1984. *Open Secret*. Putney, VT: Threshold Press. quatrain 1359.

10 Rumi. *Essential Rumi* (Coleman Barks, Transl.). San Francisco: HarperSanFrancisco. pp. 132–133.

11 Hilel Sala unpublished manuscript.

12 Ladinsky, D. 1996. *I Heard God Laughing: Renderings of Hafiz*. Walnut Creek, CA: Sufism Reoriented.

13 Frager, *op. cit*. p. 219.

Chapter Eight

1 Fadiman, James and Frager, Robert. 1997, *Essential Sufism*. San Francisco: HarperSanFrancisco. p. 89.

2 *Ibid*. p. 57.

3 Author's translation.

4 Hilel Sala, unpublished manuscript.

5 Angha, Nahid. 1995. *Deliverance: Words from the Prophet Mohammad*. San Rafael, CA: International Association of Sufism. p. 72.

6 *Ibid*. p. 27.

7 Said, Edward. 1981. *Covering Islam*. New York: Vintage. p. li.

8 Angha, *op. cit*. p. 91.

9 *Ibid*. pp. 86–87.

10 *Ibid*. p. 42.

11 Muhaiyaddeen, M. R. B. 1980. *The Truth and Unity of Man*. Philadelphia: The Fellowship Press. pp. 3–4.

12 The full text of this speech can be found at: http://www.hp.com/hpinfo/execteam/speeches/fiorina/minnesota01.htm. It was delivered at a conference on September 26, 2001 in Minneapolis, Minnesota, by Carly Fiorina, CEO, Hewlett-Packard Corporation.

GLOSSARY

Bearing Witness Entrance into Islam begins with the recitation, "I witness there is no god but God and Muhammad ﷺ is God's servant and Messenger." This is the first pillar of Islam.

Believer *Mumin* in Arabic. Someone who is sincerely and wholeheartedly devoted to living according to the teachings of the Prophets.

Dervish Someone who practices Sufism.

Fundamentalism A term often applied by Western writers to Muslims who wish to build a modern society based on Islamic rather than secular principles.

Hadith The actions and teachings of Muhammad ﷺ, which is considered second only to the Qur'an as a guide to Islamic conduct.

Heart *Qalb* in Arabic. The spiritual heart, which is the location of the soul in each human being.

Khadijah The first wife of the Prophet ﷺ and the first Muslim.

Madinah The city that took in Muhammad ﷺ and the early Muslims when they were heavily persecuted by the wealthy and powerful clans of Makkah.

Makkah The home of Muhammad ﷺ, where he first began teaching Islam, and the site of the Ka'ba, the sacred shrine toward which all Muslims pray.

Miraj The "Night-journey" of the Prophet ﷺ in which he was first taken, by the angel Gabriel, to Jerusalem and then through each of the heavens.

Muhammad ﷺ A Prophet and Messenger of God, the founder of Islam. He is considered the human embodiment of Islam.

Nafs Arabic for soul, breath, essence, or personality. A basic discipline in Sufism is the transformation of the *nafs*, from narcissism to divine unity.

Pilgrimage The observance of pilgrimage consists of a complex set of rituals and practices, including the wearing of pilgrim's garb, circling the Ka'ba, and spending a day in the desert on the plain of Arafat. It is the fifth pillar of Islam.

Prayer Formal prayer, or *salat* in Arabic, is the second pillar of Islam. Muslims are commanded to pray five times a day—at dawn, noon, mid-afternoon, dusk, and night.

Prophets Those great religious teachers who were directly inspired by God or the angels.

Qur'an The scripture of Islam; the word of God as revealed through his Prophet Muhammad ﷺ.

Ramadan The month of fasting. During this lunar month, all Muslims are commanded to abstain from eating, drinking, and making love from dawn until sundown. This practice is the third pillar of Islam.

Remembrance of God *Dhikrullah* in Arabic. The Sufi practice of repeating silently or chanting aloud Divine Names. Formal prayer is considered the best form of Remembrance.

Shariah Islamic religious law, which is based on interpretations of the teachings and doctrines found in the Qur'an and *hadith*.

Sheikh Arabic for a tribal leader, a wise elder, or teacher. A title often used for a Sufi teacher.

Soul *Ruh* in Arabic. A divine spark which was breathed from God into humanity, beginning with Adam and Eve.

Sufism The Islamic mystical tradition, which dates back well over a thousand years.

Zakat This annual charity must be given before the end of Ramadan. It is the fourth pillar of Islam.

ANNOTATED BIBLIOGRAPHY

Al-Ghazzali, M. (1983). *Inner Dimensions of Islamic Worship* (M. Holland, Trans.). London: Islamic Foundation.
A clear and concise guide to the inner meanings of the outward forms of prayer and worship in Islam, written from a Sufi perspective.

Arasteh, A. R. (1980). *Growth To Selfhood: A Sufi Contribution.* London: Routledge & Kegan Paul.
A treatise on Sufi psychology, written by an Iranian psychiatrist who is also a student of Sufism.

Armstrong, K. (2000). *Islam: A Short History.* New York: Modern Library.
An insightful and sensitive historical analysis of Islam. The book begins with the first revelation received by Muhammad ﷺ in the seventh century and concludes with a thoughtful assessment of the challenges facing Islam today.

(1992). *Muhammad: A Biography of the Prophet.* New York: HarperCollins.
An insightful and respectful portrayal of the prophet of Islam and the setting in which he lived.

Attar, Farid Ud-Din. (1961). *The Conference of the Birds* (C. S. Nott, Trans.). London: Routledge & Kegan Paul.
A classic Sufi text on the spiritual journey.

Rumi. *The Essential Rumi* (C. Barks, Trans.). San Francisco: HarperSanFrancisco.
An excellent collection of some of the world's finest mystical poetry.

Fadiman, J. & R. Frager (Eds.) (1997). *Essential Sufism.* San Francisco: HarperSanFrancisco.
The first broad-ranging, accessible exploration of the treasures of Sufism. Over three hundred beautiful and inspirational works from all eras of Sufism, from thousand-year old prayers to contemporary Sufi poetry.

Frager, R. (1999). *Heart, Self, and Soul: The Sufi Psychology of Growth, Balance, and Harmony.* Wheaton, IL: Quest Books.
The first book by a Western psychologist to explore Sufism as a path for personal growth. Full of stories, poetry, meditations, exercises and colorful everyday examples, this book will open the heart, nourish the self, and quicken the soul.

Kabir. (1977). *The Kabir Book.* Versions by Robert Bly. Boston: Beacon Press.
Wonderful, lyrical mystical poetry.

Ladinsky, D. (1996) *I Heard God Laughing: Renderings of Hafiz.* Walnut Creek, CA: Sufism Reoriented.
Marvelous renderings of the great poet Hafiz' deeply mystical, iconoclastic poetry.

Nasr, S. (1976) *Islamic Science: An Illustrated Study.* World of Islam Festival Publishing Co.
An illustrated study of Islamic science which discusses the Islamic concept of science and its transmission and classifications. Includes the Islamic sciences of cosmology, geography, mathematics, astronomy, music, physics, medicine, pharmacology, alchemy, agriculture, and various forms of technology.

Ozak, M. (al-Jerrahi). (1999). *Love Is the Wine.* (2nd Edition) (Edited and compiled by Sheikh R. Frager al-Jerrahi.) Los Angeles: Philosophical Research.
This book is derived from talks given in the United States by a contemporary Sufi master. Topics include generosity, faith, self-knowledge and love. This book presents the depths of Sufi wisdom in a modern, highly accessible form.

Ozelsel, M. (1996). *Forty Days: The Diary of a Traditional Solitary Sufi Retreat.* Brattleboro, VT: Threshold Books.
A detailed and insightful first-hand account of an extremely powerful spiritual practice-the forty day Sufi retreat. Written by a Westerner who is not only a Muslim but also a well known psychologist.

Shah, I. (1971). *The Pleasantries of the Incredible Mulla Nasrudin.* New York: Dutton.
A collection of short, funny and thought-provoking stories about Nasrudin, a folk hero who is the subject of numerous Sufi stories.

INDEX

ACKNOWLEDGEMENTS

AUTHOR ACKNOWLEDGMENTS

I have been greatly helped in the preparation of this book by the thoughtful comments of Sheikh Tosun Bayrak, Aliya Haeri, and Annick Safken. Cennet Silk has been a marvelous research assistant, and Ahmed Hussain has been a great help with Arabic. Hilel Sala was wonderfully generous with her writings and her interview material.

I would also like to thank Brenda Rosen for encouraging me to tackle this project and guiding its inception; Fiona Biggs, Debbie Thorpe, and Nicola Wright for their unstinting editorial support; Sarah Howerd and Nicola Liddiard for wonderful design; Cath Senker for her marvelous text editing; and Vanessa Fletcher for her inspired picture research.

The Bridgewater Book Company would like to thank the following:
The Islamic Texts Society, 22a Brooklands Avenue, Cambridge CB2 2DQ, UK.
Telephone: 01223 314387. email: mail@its.org.uk.
The Muslim Directory. Telephone: 0208 8400020

PICTURE ACKNOWLEDGMENTS

The Bridgewater Book Company would also like to thank the following for permission to reproduce copyright material:

CORBIS:pps. 7 Sergio Dorantes, 12 Michael S Yamashita, 13 Dean Conger, 14 David Turnley, 15 Michael Garrett, 16 Nik Wheeler, 18 David Rubinger, 20 Annie Griffiths Belt, 21 Margaret Courtney-Clarke, 22 & 23 David Turnley, 24 Sandro Vannini, 26/27 Adam Woolfitt, 29 Juan Echeverria, 30 Yann Arthus Bertrand, 31 Kevin Fleming, 35 Francois de Mulder, 36/37 David Turnley, 40/41 Bojan Brecelj, 47 Earl and Nazima Kowall, 48 Charles and Josette Lenars, 49 Steve Satushek, 50 Mark Lewis, 52/53 Angelo Hornak, 56 Wolfgang Kaehler, 59 Richard T Nowitz, 60 Roger Antrobus, 61 Vanni Archive, 71 K M Westermann, 72 Dave Bartruff, 74 Lloyd Cluff, 76 K M Westermann, 78 David Turnley, 80 Lindsay Hebberd, 82 Ed Kashi, 84 David Webb, 86 Annie Griffiths Belt, 87 Dave Bartruff, 88 Neil Rabinowitz, 93 Paul Almasy, 94/95 Sandro Vannini, 97 David Turnley, 98 Roger Wood, 102 & 103 David H Wells, 104 Richard Powell, 105 Caroline Penn, 107 Adam Woolfitt, 109 Ed Kashi, 111 Kevin Fleming, 114 Lindsay Hebberd, 117 Peter Turnley, 118 Charles and Josette Lenars, 121 Peter Turnley, 122/123 Lindsay Hebberd, 124 Chris Hellier, 126 Bettmann, 128 Owen Franken, 129 Bettmann, 130 Angelo Hornak, 133 Bettmann, 134 Ann Palma, 135 David Turnley, 137 Farrel Grehan. GETTY IMAGES: pps.10/11 & 17 Nabeel Turner /Stone, 19 Owen Franken/Stone, 38 Navada Wier/The Image Bank, 39 Guido Alberto Rossi/The Image Bank, 49 Steve Satushek/The Image Bank, 50 Mark Lewis/Stone, SARAH HOWERD: p.90.